YOUR STORY HAS A VILLAIN

PUT ON THE ARMOR OF GOD EACH DAY

BIBLE STUDY GUIDE | FIVE SESSIONS

JONATHAN "JP" POKLUDA

WITH SAM O'NEAL

HarperChristian
Resources

Your Story Has a Villain Study Guide
© 2024 by Jonathan Pokluda

Published in Grand Rapids, Michigan, by HarperChristian Resources. HarperChristian Resources is a registered trademark of HarperCollins Christian Publishing, Inc.

Requests for information should be sent to customercare@harpercollins.com.

ISBN 978-0-310-16982-6 (softcover)
ISBN 978-0-310-16983-3 (ebook)

All Scripture quotations are taken from the Holy Bible, New International Version®, NIV®. Copyright © 1973, 1978, 1984, 2011 by Biblica, Inc.® Used by permission. All rights reserved worldwide.

Any internet addresses (websites, blogs, etc.) and telephone numbers in this study guide are offered as a resource. They are not intended in any way to be or imply an endorsement by HarperChristian Resources, nor does HarperChristian Resources vouch for the content of these sites and numbers for the life of this study guide.

HarperChristian Resources titles may be purchased in bulk for church, business, fundraising, or ministry use. For information, please e-mail ResourceSpecialist@ChurchSource.com.

First Printing December 2024 / Printed in the United States of America

CONTENTS

A NOTE FROM JONATHAN

Have you noticed that villains have been having a moment in recent years? I'm talking mostly about the entertainment industry, including books, movies, and TV shows. The bad guys in a lot of our favorite stories have become less "forces of evil" and more "it's complicated."

Just look at Loki. He was the unquestioned villain of the first *Avengers* movie when it came out in 2012. He came to earth trying to pick a fight with his older brother, Thor, and establish himself as a ruling force in the universe. He was more than willing to kill millions of people to achieve his goals, and he unleashed an invading force of aliens to take what he wanted by force. So, Loki was clearly not a good guy. Not even a complex character.

However, by 2021, Loki had his own show where he was . . . the *good guy*. He became the dedicated protagonist willing to sacrifice himself for the safety of others. Sure, this Loki was an alternate "time-variant" version of his original self, but still, the premise is that the evil Loki (in whatever version of himself was now present) was now the *hero*.[1]

I know this is just one example, but if you've been paying attention to the entertainment world over the last decade or so, you have likely noticed that the lines between good and evil have become blurred in this way. Evil characters have become more complex . . . some, like Loki, have even become noble. At the same time, good characters have become more nuanced, and some even reckless and criminal. (I'm looking at you, Deadpool.)

The evolution of villains in our popular culture may make for more interesting storylines, but it can create a lot of confusion about our real world and our real lives. The reason for this is because the Bible tells us that there is a *real* villain in our story. There is a real "bad guy" who is seeking to "steal and kill and destroy" the world and our lives (John 10:10).

This villain is not complex. He does not have misunderstood motives. No, his objectives are clear—and they are pure evil. He is active in our world today . . . and he is not alone. Yes, our story has a villain, and his name is Satan. My goal for this study is to help you better grasp what you need to know about this villain and what you can do to reject him and resist him each day.

— JONATHAN "JP" POKLUDA

HOW TO USE THIS GUIDE

We have all heard about the villain in our story, even though we all use a lot of different names to describe him: Satan, the serpent, Lucifer, the devil, the dragon, "the ruler of the kingdom of the air" (Ephesians 2:2).[2] No matter what you call him, the stark reality is that there is a villain out there who is personally interested in your destruction, in your family's destruction, in your community's destruction, and in your nation's destruction.

This is why we are going to spend the next several weeks exploring this villain and how you can "suit up" to fight against him. The stakes in this battle are high, but thankfully, you are not in the fight alone. You don't have to struggle against the villain of your story using your own resources—your own brains, brawn, and bills. No, you have access to *heavenly* resources. As a follower of Jesus, you have been given everything you need to demolish every attack, destroy every accusation, and defeat the Enemy of your story.

Before you begin this study, keep in mind that there are a few ways you can go through this material. You can experience this study with others in a group (such as a Bible study, Sunday school class, or any other small-group gathering), or you may choose to go through the content on your own. Either way, know that the videos for each session are available for you to view at any time via streaming by following the instructions that have been provided with this study guide.

GROUP STUDY

Each session in *Your Story Has a Villain* is divided into two parts: (1) a group study section and (2) a personal study section. The group study section provides a basic framework on how to open your time together, get the most out of the video content, and discuss the key ideas that were presented in the teaching. Each session includes the following:

- **Welcome:** A short opening note about the topic of the session for you to read on your own before you meet as a group.
- **Connect:** A few icebreaker questions to get you and your group members thinking about the topic and interacting with each other.
- **Watch:** An outline of the key points covered in each video teaching along with space for you to take notes as you watch each session.
- **Discuss:** Questions to help you and your group reflect on the teaching material presented and apply it to your lives.
- **Respond:** A short personal exercise to help reinforce the key ideas.
- **Pray:** A few ideas for how to close out your group time in prayer.

If you are doing this study in a group, make sure that you have your own copy of the study guide so you can write down your thoughts, responses, and reflections—and so you have access to the videos via streaming. You will also want to have a copy of the book *Your Story Has a Villain*, as reading it alongside this guide will provide you with deeper insights. (See the notes at the beginning of each group session and personal study section on which chapters of the book you should read before the next group session.)

Finally, keep these points in mind:

- **Facilitation:** If you are doing this study in a group, you will want to appoint someone to serve as a facilitator. This person will be responsible for starting the video and keeping track of time during discussions and activities. If *you* have been chosen for this role, there are some resources in the back of this guide that can help you lead your group through the study.

- **Faithfulness:** Your group is a place where tremendous growth can happen as you reflect on the Bible, ask questions, and learn what God is doing in other people's lives. For this reason, be fully committed and attend each session so you can build trust and rapport with the other members.

- **Friendship:** The goal of any small group is to serve as a place where people can share, learn about God, and build friendships. So seek to make your group a "safe place." Be honest about your thoughts and feelings but also listen carefully to everyone else's thoughts, feelings, and opinions. Keep anything personal that your group members share in confidence so that you can create a community where people can heal, be challenged, and grow spiritually.

If you are going through this study on your own, read the opening Welcome section and reflect on the questions in the Connect section. Watch the video and use the prompts provided to take notes. Finally, personalize the questions and exercises in the Discuss and Respond sections. Close by writing down any requests that you want to pray about during the upcoming week.

PERSONAL STUDY

The personal study is for you to work through on your own during the week. Each exercise is designed to help you explore the key ideas you uncovered during your group time and delve into passages of Scripture that will help you apply those principles to your life. Go at your own pace, doing a little each day—or tackle the material all at once. Remember to spend a few moments in silence to listen to whatever God might be saying to you.

Note that if you are doing this study as part of a group, and you are unable to finish (or even start) these personal studies for the week, you should still attend the group time. Be assured that you are still wanted and welcome even if you don't have your "homework" done. The group studies and personal studies are intended to help you hear what God wants you to hear and learn how to apply what He is saying to your life. So . . . as you go through this study, be listening for Him to speak to you about standing against the villain in your story.

WEEK 1

BEFORE GROUP MEETING	Read the introduction and chapters 1–3 in *Your Story Has a Villain* Read the Welcome section (page 2)
GROUP MEETING	Discuss the Connect questions Watch the video teaching for session 1 Discuss the questions that follow as a group Do the closing exercise and pray (pages 2–6)
STUDY 1	Complete the personal study (pages 9–12)
STUDY 2	Complete the personal study (pages 13–16)
STUDY 3	Complete the personal study (pages 17–20)
CATCH UP AND READ AHEAD (BEFORE WEEK 2 GROUP MEETING)	Connect with someone in your group Read chapters 4–5 in *Your Story Has a Villain* Complete any unfinished personal studies (page 21)

KNOW THE VILLAIN IN YOUR STORY

Put on the full armor of God, so that you can take your stand against the devil's schemes. For our struggle is not against flesh and blood, but against the rulers, against the authorities, against the powers of this dark world and against the spiritual forces of evil in the heavenly realms.

EPHESIANS 6:11–12

WELCOME | READ ON YOUR OWN

There are a lot of ugly words in our world today. The type of words that get people canceled when they are posted on social media or unearthed from decades-old video clips. Words that try to reduce whole swathes of people down to ignorant and insulting stereotypes. (Obviously we are not going to list any of those words here, because doing so would be about the worst way to start the first session of a Bible study. But you know what we're talking about here.)

Yet there is one ugly word we need to call out, because it is one we don't think about often: *apathy.* Why is that an ugly word? Because, when applied to our spiritual lives, it is more common than we think and more dangerous than we know.

Imagine that you are with your family and you get one of those government-alert texts: "A dangerous lion has escaped from the zoo in your immediate location. Take shelter and be alert." Can you imagine receiving that text and then just strolling down the street with your loved ones as if nothing were happening? Wouldn't that be crazy? It would represent negligence on a major scale when it comes to your responsibility to protect yourself and those you love from a dangerous threat.

Apathy in the face of real and present danger would be a terrible decision. Yet as followers of Jesus, we demonstrate a similar kind of apathy (and negligence) each day. We read the many warnings that God gives us in the Bible—but then choose to do nothing about them.

CONNECT | 10 MINUTES

If any of your group members don't know each other, take a few minutes to introduce yourselves. Then discuss one of the following questions:

- Why did you decide to join this Bible study? What do you hope to learn or experience as you go through it?

  — *or* —

- On a scale of 1 (low) to 10 (high), how would you rate your interest in spiritual warfare? Explain as you are able.

WATCH | 25 MINUTES

Watch the video for this session, which you can access by playing the DVD or through streaming (see the instructions provided with this study guide). As you watch, use the following outline to record any thoughts or concepts that stand out to you.

OUTLINE

I. There are three common errors when it comes to how people approach Satan.
   A. *Disbelief*: We don't recognize the reality of evil.
   B. *Obsession*: We think about evil and demonic forces way too much.
   C. *Apathy*: We believe in the reality of evil but don't think it affects our lives.

II. Paul gives us insights about the villain in our story in Ephesians 6:10–13.
   A. Paul says that God is the source of our strength for defeating the devil.
   B. The Lord gives us spiritual protection against the Enemy's attacks: the "full armor of God."
   C. The Enemy in our lives is not a political party, or a neighbor, or a family member, or any other person. The Enemy is Satan and his "forces of evil."

III. The Bible reveals that Satan is a fallen angel.
   A. Angels were created beings made to worship God.
   B. However, Lucifer (or Satan) didn't want to *worship* God but to *be* like God (see Isaiah 14:13).
   C. Satan and one-third of the angels who followed him were cast down (see Revelation 12:7–9).
   D. Satan thus commands a large number of demons and has been given power and authority in our world—and even in our lives through temptation.

IV. The reality is that we never *have* to sin.
   A. We will never be in a situation where choice 1 is to sin or choice 2 is to sin.
   B. Paul tells us in 1 Corinthians 10:13 that there is always a path for resisting the Enemy.
   C. What we need to know is that a spirit of selfishness is a satanic spirit.

V. The Bible reveals that God is greater than Satan.
   A. In Genesis 3:15, God promised that Jesus would ultimately defeat Satan.
   B. Jesus and Satan are not equal forces locked in a duel. Jesus is sovereign over Satan and has power over him. Satan is no match for Christ.
   C. However, Satan is still a force in our world today, so we need to know who he is and exactly what he is capable of doing.

NOTES

DISCUSS | 35 MINUTES

Now discuss what you just watched by answering the following questions.

1. As you get started with this study, what can you say for certain about the villain in your story? What are some facts or truths you believe are 100 percent accurate when it comes to the devil? Where did you learn those facts or truths?

2. Ask someone to read Ephesians 6:10–13. When you hear these verses, what important words or phrases catch your attention? Why those words or phrases?

3. The apostle Paul makes it clear that Satan *does* have power in our world and even in our lives as individuals. He leads "the powers of this dark world" (verse 12). What are some possible reasons why God has allowed the devil to demonstrate such authority here and now?

4. Ask someone to read aloud 1 Corinthians 15:51–57. We often think of Jesus and Satan as opposites—as two powerful forces vying for control of humanity. The reality is that Satan is merely a created being. He is a fallen angel, while Jesus is all-powerful. What are some practical ways we can remind ourselves of this truth that Satan is not equal with Christ?

5. Satan has a major role to play in the suffering that people experience all over the world—but we also contribute our own negative consequences when we choose to sin against God. How should believers in Christ understand the balance between Satan's work and their own sinfulness? Which one has the greater influence in our lives?

RESPOND | 10 MINUTES

One of the great things about the Bible is that it reveals truths that we otherwise would have no way of figuring out on our own. This is the case when it comes to Satan. God's Word has a lot to say about our Enemy, the devil, and we're going to cover many important passages in the course of this study. But to get started, take a look at Isaiah 14:12–15, which was mentioned in the teaching. On the one hand, these verses refer to the downfall of Babylon's king, yet on a different layer, they also offer specific insights into the being we call Satan.

> [12] How you have fallen from heaven, morning star, son of the dawn! You have been cast down to the earth, you who once laid low the nations! [13] You said in your heart, "I will ascend to the heavens; I will raise my throne above the stars of God; I will sit enthroned on the mount of assembly, on the utmost heights of Mount Zaphon. [14] I will ascend above the tops of the clouds; I will make myself like the Most High." [15] But you are brought down to the realm of the dead.
>
> **ISAIAH 14:12–15**

What do you learn from these verses about who Satan is and what he wants?

What are lessons you've learned when it comes to resisting Satan?

PRAY | 10 MINUTES

When it is time to close, join as a group to pray for God's blessings over this course. Be intentional about repenting of any apathy currently in your life when it comes to Satan, the reality of evil, and the impact of temptation in your life. Ask that God would pour out wisdom and clarity over the group as you tackle these subjects together. Before you end, write down any requests from yourself or the group so you and your fellow group members can continue to pray about them in the week ahead.

PERSONAL STUDY

You are at the start of a study on Satan, sin, and the reality of evil not just in the world but also in your life. Without a doubt, the Bible is the best resource for information on those topics. So, in the personal study portion of each session, you will take a deeper look at specific passages and principles in God's Word that are the most helpful for exposing and resisting the villain in your story. As you work through each of these exercises, be sure to write down your responses to the questions, as you will be given a few minutes to share your insights and key takeaways at the start of the next session. If you are reading *Your Story Has a Villain* alongside this study, first review the introduction and chapters 1–3 in the book.

Satan himself masquerades as an angel of light.

1 CORINTHIANS 11:14

WELCOME TO HELL

In the same way that many people in our culture (including believers) often feel apathy about the reality of Satan, many also feel apathy regarding the question of hell. Or maybe we should say *questions*: Is hell a real place? Does God really send people to hell? Is there any way to get out of hell once we find ourselves there?

These types of concerns used to spur a lot of passion in the hearts of people. A lot of disquiet and debate. But now we often shrug our shoulders. "God is love, so I feel pretty confident that everything will work out."

So, let's get a few important things out of the way here at the beginning of this study. First, as we stressed during the group time, *Satan is real*. He is a *real* being who is alive, deeply malevolent, and hatefully motivated to destroy everything good in this world—including you and your family. Satan is a spiritual being, not a physical being, which means he doesn't walk around in a body. But he carries authority within our world to accomplish his will.

Second, *hell is real*. Now, it is true that we do not know if hell exists as a geographical location somewhere in space or only as a spiritual realm, but we do know that it exists. This is because the Bible has an awful lot to say about hell, including this verse: "God did not spare angels when they sinned, but sent them to hell, putting them in chains of darkness to be held for judgment" (2 Peter 2:4). We will explore a few more passages in the pages to come, but Scripture is clear that hell is not a myth or an allegory or a made-up idea. It's *real*.

So, what does the reality that both Satan and hell actually exist mean for followers of Jesus? It means that we have a choice. We can continue to ignore these realities and hope they don't have any significant impact on our everyday lives. Or—better choice—we can learn everything we can about hell, the devil, and his goals for our lives so we can put ourselves in the best position possible to resist and reject the Enemy at every possible turn.

1. In a typical week, how often do you think about Satan, his forces (demons), or hell? How often do you think about anything related to the fact that there is a spiritual realm?

Satan and his forces:

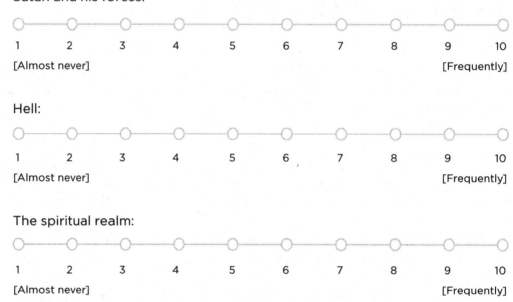

1	2	3	4	5	6	7	8	9	10

[Almost never]   [Frequently]

Hell:

1	2	3	4	5	6	7	8	9	10

[Almost never]   [Frequently]

The spiritual realm:

1	2	3	4	5	6	7	8	9	10

[Almost never]   [Frequently]

2. A 2022 study conducted by Ligonier Ministries and Lifeway Research found that 29 percent of evangelicals in the United States did not believe hell is a real place where people will be punished forever.[3] Why do you think people have a hard time accepting the reality that there is a hell? What are some questions or objections you have heard from fellow Christians?

We need to understand an important concept: Hell is a subtraction. It is subtracting out the goodness of God. When you have light and you subtract light, you are left with darkness. When you have comfort and you subtract comfort, you are left with pain. Anything good in this world comes from God. James, the half brother of Jesus, even wrote that in the Scriptures, saying, "Every good and perfect gift is from above, coming down from the Father of the heavenly lights" (James 1:17). When you subtract the Father of heavenly lights, the goodness of God, you are left with only evil.[4]

3. Read John 8:12, 1 John 1:5, and 2 Corinthians 1:1-4. These verses proclaim that Jesus is the light of the world, that there is no darkness at all in God, and that God the Father and Jesus Christ comforts us in our troubles. Now imagine a place where these things do not exist. How do you envision it would be if all of God's goodness were subtracted from existence?

[43] "If your hand causes you to stumble, cut it off. It is better for you to enter life maimed than with two hands to go into hell, where the fire never goes out. [44] [45] And if your foot causes you to stumble, cut it off. It is better for you to enter life crippled than to have two feet and be thrown into hell. [46] [47] And if your eye causes you to stumble, pluck it out. It is better for you to enter the kingdom of God with one eye than to have two eyes and be thrown into hell, where 'the worms that eat them do not die, and the fire is not quenched.' Everyone will be salted with fire" (Mark 9:43-49).

4. In the passage you just read on the previous page, **underline** or **circle** each time Jesus says it is better to cut off or pluck out a certain body part than endure the fires of hell. Based on the examples he uses in this passage, what message is he communicating to his followers about not ending up in hell?

5. "Every single person you know—every person you've ever interacted with, and every person who has ever lived—will be in either heaven or hell one day, forever."[5] As you consider this truth, what are your goals in participating in this study? What do you hope to learn to better help those in your world understand the reality of both heaven and hell?

MISTAKEN IDENTITY

We all love a good origin story. Whether it is a hero or a villain, we like to learn the backstory of important characters. We want to know what events pushed them into their chosen path and what decisions are driving them as they work to save the world or destroy the world.

It is interesting that the Bible offers an origin story for Satan. He appears for the first time right at the beginning of Scripture—Genesis 3, to be precise—where he functions as the villain of the story by convincing the first human beings, Adam and Eve, to sin. It is obvious from that chapter in Genesis that Satan, the serpent, is a big deal and will be a bad influence in the story that follows.

But how did Satan *become* Satan? What caused him to choose the path of evil rather than good? In other words, what is his origin story? We find the answer in Ezekiel.

This book was written by a prophet named (you guessed it) Ezekiel during the years when Israel as a nation was harassed and, ultimately, conquered by Babylon. The overall theme of Ezekiel's prophecy is the failure of God's chosen people to worship Him rather than idols—to follow His will rather than their own way.

It is kind of fitting, then, that in the middle of that prophecy (Ezekiel 28) comes a detailed exploration of how Satan became the devil. Here is a portion of that chapter: "So I drove you in disgrace from the mount of God, and I expelled you, guardian cherub, from among the fiery stones. Your heart became proud on account of your beauty, and you corrupted your wisdom because of your splendor. So I threw you to the earth; I made a spectacle of you before kings" (verses 16–17).

We will explore this chapter in the book of Ezekiel in more detail during today's study, but here is the TL;DR version.[6] God created Satan to be a creature of worship who would *reflect* glory to Himself, but Satan chose to be a creature *seeking* worship who coveted glory for himself. As a result, Satan was cast out of heaven and became the villain of our stories here on earth.

1. In your own words, how would you describe the benefits of understanding Satan's "origin story"? How does that knowledge help us in our everyday lives?

2. Satan and his forces have goals for your life. They have choices they want you to make and paths they want you to follow. Take a moment to think about this reality. In the table below, list some of the choices that Satan might be tempting you to make today, and then list the life path he might be tempting you to follow over the next six months.

How Satan is tempting me today	What path he might want me to follow

3. Ezekiel spoke a lament over "the king of Tyre," who was a contemporary ruler of his day. But his prophecy also digs deeper into spiritual darkness. Read the following passage and then **circle** any words or phrases that point to Satan as a subject of this lament.

> [12] "You were the seal of perfection,
>   full of wisdom and perfect in beauty.
> [13] You were in Eden,
>   the garden of God;
> every precious stone adorned you:
>   carnelian, chrysolite and emerald,
>   topaz, onyx and jasper,
>   lapis lazuli, turquoise and beryl.
> Your settings and mountings were made of gold;
>   on the day you were created they were prepared.
> [14] You were anointed as a guardian cherub,
>   for so I ordained you.
> You were on the holy mount of God;
>   you walked among the fiery stones.
> [15] You were blameless in your ways
>   from the day you were created
>   till wickedness was found in you.
> [16] Through your widespread trade
>   you were filled with violence,
>   and you sinned.
> So I drove you in disgrace from the mount of God,
>   and I expelled you, guardian cherub,
>   from among the fiery stones."

> **EZEKIEL 28:12–16**

Take a look at the words and phrases you circled in this passage. What did you learn about the devil?

4. Satan and his demons rebelled against God because they wanted to control and receive worship themselves rather than submit and offer worship to God. Where do you feel tempted to retain control over your life rather than submit to God's will? (Be honest!)

Read this carefully: you and I are in the test. Who are you going to worship? God, the Creator of the heavens and the earth, or the prince of this era? Paul referred to Satan as the "god of this age" in 2 Corinthians 4:4, meaning Satan is actively involved in the here and now of daily life. So, which way will you go? Every day we have to choose.

Here is the most mind-bending part of all this: you can sit in church on a Sunday morning and worship Satan. We think of satanism as something way different, but the truth is, he does not need you to worship him with Ouija boards, seances, lit candles, and sacrifices.

When you worship *anything other than God*, Satan will accept that as worship to himself. In fact, he would probably prefer that you do not even waste your time with the Ouija boards and candles, because that's weird, and then you would not have friends, and therefore you would have no influence. What he really wants you to do is worship anything other than God and influence as many others as possible to do the same. This is his tactic, and he carries it out every day here on earth.[7]

5. Where do you see your culture pushing people to worship things other than God? Where are you currently elevating something (or someone) to a place that is higher than God?

AN INVISIBLE ARMY

If you've watched *The Lord of the Rings: Return of the King*, you may remember the scene where the huge hordes of orcs surround the capital city of Gondor.[8] The scene itself is crazy.

In the film, you see a brilliant city called Minas Tirith that is built in incredible layers of white stone against a mountain. Several rings of white walls scale upward and inward, and a majestic-looking spike juts out from the top of the city (almost like the prow of a sailboat). This represents the kingdom of Gondor, which in the story has all the good guys inside.

Yet there is another kingdom represented in the battle, which is the kingdom of Sauron—the bad guy. His armies surround the walls of the city. In the movie, you see ranks upon ranks of these hideous creatures called orcs. Honestly, they look demonic—probably similar to what most of us visualize in our minds when we think about demons. There are millions of these evil creatures literally piled up around the white walls of Minas Tirith.

In many ways, this scene illustrates in a visceral way what we are really up against as citizens of God's kingdom currently living in this world. We are in a fight. We are in a war against a real and present danger in the form of Satan and his demonic forces. Remember the words of author and theologian C. S. Lewis: "There is no neutral ground in the universe. Every square inch, every split second is claimed by God, and counterclaimed by Satan."[9]

We need to face this fact if we are going to survive and thrive in the context of spiritual warfare. This is why it's important for us to spend time and energy learning about the forces of evil. So far, we've covered the reality of Satan and hell. Now it's time to take a closer look at demons and how they influence not just our world as a whole but also our lives as individuals.

1. The concept of demons is often viewed as "too much" for Christians—too far from polite conversation or rational belief. Despite that hurdle, what have you been taught about the nature, goals, and practices of demons in our world?

2. When have you personally encountered a situation, person, or experience that felt "demonic"? What about it made it feel that way to you?

> [1] They went across the lake to the region of the Gerasenes. [2] When Jesus got out of the boat, a man with an impure spirit came from the tombs to meet him. [3] This man lived in the tombs, and no one could bind him anymore, not even with a chain. [4] For he had often been chained hand and foot, but he tore the chains apart and broke the irons on his feet. No one was strong enough to subdue him. [5] Night and day among the tombs and in the hills he would cry out and cut himself with stones.
>
> [6] When he saw Jesus from a distance, he ran and fell on his knees in front of him. [7] He shouted at the top of his voice, "What do you want with me, Jesus, Son of the Most High God? In God's name don't torture me!" [8] For Jesus had said to him, "Come out of this man, you impure spirit!"
>
> [9] Then Jesus asked him, "What is your name?"
>
> "My name is Legion," he replied, "for we are many." [10] And he begged Jesus again and again not to send them out of the area" (Mark 5:1–10).

3. Review what this passage says about the man inhabited by demons (verses 1–5) and the demons themselves (verses 6–10). On the following chart, write down **four things** this passage says about the man and his actions and **two things** the demons request of Jesus.

The man:

Where did he live?

How had he been restrained?

What had he done with these restraints?

What would he do night and day?

The demons:

What did the demons first ask Jesus?

What did the demons beg of Jesus?

4. One thing that is clear throughout the Gospels is that Jesus has *authority* over Satan and all demons. He effortlessly demonstrates power over the forces of evil at every turn. So, what specific steps can you take to apply that authority and power in your life?

I believe that every human being is influenced by a spirit: either demonic spirits or the Holy Spirit. The world is first spiritual, and every human interaction in the world has spiritual implications. There is an army of evil beings trying to keep every human away from God. If we're not being influenced by the Holy Spirit, we are certainly being influenced by evil spirits. Scripture never explicitly says that Christians (who all have the Holy Spirit dwelling inside of them) cannot be possessed by demons or evil spirits, but I understand why many jump to that conclusion. In my humble opinion, we make up different labels like *possession* and *oppression* to describe what the Enemy can do. Whenever demonic possession occurs in the New Testament, it is happening in an unbeliever. However, Christians can be *influenced* by demonic spirits, which is why we are instructed to resist the devil and his forces (1 Peter 5:8–9; James 4:7).[10]

5. Read John 16:12–15. In the same way that it is important for us to understand who demons are and how they work in order to defeat them, we must also understand who the Holy Spirit is and how He operates in order to gain the most benefit from his presence. What are some of the ways the Holy Spirit interacts with your life, your thoughts, and your decisions?

CATCH UP AND READ AHEAD

Take time today to connect with a group member and talk about some of the insights from this session. Use any of the prompts below to help guide your discussion.

- What have you liked best from the content in this session, including both the group study and personal study? Why?
- How comfortable do you feel talking about subjects like Satan, hell, and demons? Why do you feel that way?
- What have you learned about Satan and/or demons this week that is new to you? What information has been especially helpful?
- Satan and his forces want us to make choices that move us away from God. How can you keep that reality in the front of your mind each day?
- What do you feel most excited to explore or learn in the sessions ahead?

Use this time to go back and complete any of the study and reflection questions from previous days that you weren't able to finish. Make a note below of any revelations you've had and reflect on any growth or personal insights you've gained.

Read chapters 4 and 6 in *Your Story Has a Villain* before the next group session. Use the space below to note anything that stands out to you or encourages you.

WEEK 2

BEFORE GROUP MEETING	Read chapters 4 and 6 in *Your Story Has a Villain* Read the Welcome section (page 24)
GROUP MEETING	Discuss the Connect questions Watch the video teaching for session 2 Discuss the questions that follow as a group Do the closing exercise and pray (pages 24–28)
STUDY 1	Complete the personal study (pages 31–34)
STUDY 2	Complete the personal study (pages 35–38)
STUDY 3	Complete the personal study (pages 39–42)
CATCH UP AND READ AHEAD (BEFORE WEEK 3 GROUP MEETING)	Connect with someone in your group Read chapters 5 and 7 in *Your Story Has a Villain* Complete any unfinished personal studies (page 43)

GRASP GOD'S TRUTH AND RIGHTEOUSNESS

Stand firm then, with the belt of truth buckled around your waist, with the breastplate of righteousness in place.

EPHESIANS 6:14

WELCOME | READ ON YOUR OWN

Plate armor reached its peak during the fifteenth and sixteenth centuries in Europe.[11] Maybe you've seen one of these suits of armor in a museum, or in the movies, or in paintings or illustrations. When you look at them, you can get the sense that they were a complete shell of some kind. Almost as if the knight could undo a few clasps on the armor, step inside like putting on a pair of pants, and then seal everything up.

But the reality was much different. These ancient suits of armor were not a single item but were made up of several different pieces that all fit together to create the semblance of something joined together. If you were a knight, you would have worn a helmet to cover your head, a gorget to cover your throat, pauldrons to protect your shoulders, vambraces to cover your forearms, gauntlets for your hands, greaves for your legs, sabatons for your feet, plus a separate layer of chain mail to cover all the gaps left by all those other pieces of armor.[12]

In short, it took a lot of specialized pieces to form an effective suit of armor. The same is true of the armor on which we rely in our spiritual lives—what people for centuries have called "the armor of God." God's armor does not come as a single piece. Instead, our protection is the result of several specialized pieces fitting together into a cohesive unit to cover those parts of our hearts and minds that are most valuable and most vulnerable to the Enemy. We are going to explore each of these parts of armor over the next several sessions. We will begin by examining two critical pieces: the **belt of truth** and **breastplate of righteousness**.

CONNECT | 10 MINUTES

Take a few minutes to get better acquainted with fellow members. Then choose one of the following questions to discuss as a group:

- What is something that resonated with you in last week's personal study that you would like to share with the group?

  — or —

- When do you remember reading or hearing about "the armor of God" for the first time? How did you think that armor was supposed to work?

WATCH | 25 MINUTES

Now watch the video for this session. Below is an outline of the key points covered during the teaching. Record any key concepts that stand out to you.

OUTLINE

I. We are called to stand against Satan's attacks by donning the first two pieces of spiritual armor:
   A. "The *belt of truth* buckled around your waist" (Ephesians 6:14a).
   B. "The *breastplate of righteousness* in place" (Ephesians 6:14b).

II. Satan tries to take things that are valuable and make them look cheap.
   A. Specifically, Satan's evil forces try to take the expensive things of God and made them look cheap and try to take the cheap things of this world and make them look expensive.
   B. Demonic forces often operate like a group of mischievous teenagers. They are focused on distracting us from God's righteous calling on our lives.
   C. For this reason, we are to "gird our loins" with the truth.

III. The belt of truth will enable us to protect our thoughts from Satan's *lies*.
   A. Satan began his connection with humanity by lying to Adam and Eve (see Genesis 3).
   B. Satan still tries to convince us today that God is holding back good things from us.
   C. When we know the truth of God's Word, we can counter Satan's lies.

IV. The breastplate of righteousness will enable us to protect our *hearts* from Satan's attacks.
   A. The breastplate is critical because it protects us from lethal blows to the heart.
   B. The type of righteousness that Paul is referring to is called *sanctifying righteousness.*
   C. This is the kind of righteousness that we pursue as we surrender to the spirit of God.

V. Satan wants us to compromise, but God calls us to a life of integrity.
   A. We need to remember in all our dealings that we represent God's kingdom.
   B. We are God's ambassadors on this earth (see 2 Corinthians 5:20).
   C. We need to trust in the Lord (see Proverbs 3:5) and guard our hearts (see Proverbs 4:23).

NOTES

DISCUSS | 35 MINUTES

Now discuss what you just watched by answering the following questions.

1. Begin by discussing the questions that were raised at the end of this week's teaching: What lies of the Enemy are you believing right now? What is the Enemy making look valuable when it's actually cheap and of this world? How will you commit to walking in the righteousness of Jesus?

2. Jesus said "there is no truth" in Satan and that "when he lies, he speaks his native language, for he is a liar and the father of lies" (John 8:44). What are some of the biggest lies that our culture has chosen to promote in recent years? How would you assess the damage that has been caused because of these lies?

3. The belt that the Roman soldiers wore in Paul's day was called the balteus. It was the first article of armor they put on, and it ended with several throngs with metal fittings that served to protect sensitive parts of the body. The Roman soldier would strap a sword to this belt when he went into battle. How does this description reveal the importance that Paul put on God's truth? Why is truth foundational to the other pieces of spiritual armor?

4. Paul states that we are next to put on the "breastplate of righteousness" (Ephesians 6:14). As noted in this teaching, Paul is referring to something known as *sanctifying righteousness.* Ask someone to read aloud 1 Peter 1:14–16. According to this passage, what does it mean to walk in this kind of righteousness? What does it mean to pursue a "holy" life?

5. Ask someone to read aloud 2 Corinthians 5:21. One of the profound truths of the gospel is that Jesus not only *takes away* our sin in the process we call salvation but also *gives* us something—His righteousness. What is the difference between confronting Satan with our own righteousness versus confronting him with Christ's righteousness?

RESPOND | 10 MINUTES

During Jesus' public ministry, He was often confronted by the Jewish religious leaders of the day. On one occasion, these leaders made a big deal of claiming they were children of Abraham—Hebrews by blood and through their worship of God. Jesus countered their claims by revealing they were descendants of someone else when it came to their preference for lies over truth:

> [42] Jesus said to them, "If God were your Father, you would love me, for I have come here from God. I have not come on my own; God sent me. [43] Why is my language not clear to you? Because you are unable to hear what I say. [44] You belong to your father, the devil, and you want to carry out your father's desires. He was a murderer from the beginning, not holding to the truth, for there is no truth in him. . . . [47] Whoever belongs to God hears what God says. The reason you do not hear is that you do not belong to God."
>
> **JOHN 8:42–44, 47**

What did Jesus say these religious leaders would do if God were truly their Father? What lies from Satan were they believing that caused them to not recognize Jesus for who He was?

How can we tell when we are listening to Satan's lies rather than staying focused on the truth? What are some symptoms that can help us recognize when we are being deceived?

PRAY | 10 MINUTES

Conclude this session by affirming your belief that God is the source of all truth—that whatever God declares to be true is true indeed, regardless of what the world around us may say. Express gratitude to Jesus that you have been covered by His righteousness because of His death on the cross. Commit to equipping yourself with the belt of truth and the breastplate of righteousness each day as you seek to serve Him.

PERSONAL STUDY

We covered several foundational truths of spiritual warfare in the first session. Namely, we saw that Satan is real, hell is real, and demons are real and active in our world. In other words, each of us has a villain in our story—one who desires to destroy us. In the group section of this session, you began to unpack some of the tools God has given you to take a stand against Satan, starting with the belt of truth and the breastplate of righteousness. In this week's personal study, you will take a deeper look at how Satan operates and what he seeks to accomplish by attacking your heart and mind with his lies. As you work through these exercises, again write down your responses to the questions, as you will be given a few minutes to share your insights and key takeaways at the start of the next session. If you are reading *Your Story Has a Villain* alongside this study, first review chapters 4 and 6 in the book.

Let us not love with words or speech but with actions and in truth.

1 JOHN 3:18

WHAT THE VILLAIN DOES

Here's a question worth considering: *How would the Enemy take you out?* Put your-self in Satan's shoes for minute. (Yes, this is an unpleasant thought, but try.) If you were Satan, and you were trying to destroy *you*, where would you start the attack? What vulnerabilities would you exploit? What weaknesses would you target? What areas of pride would you inflame?

In short, if you had to come up with a plan to destroy yourself, what would be the first three items on that list? It is certainly worth giving a few minutes of your time to con-sider, because the truth of the matter is that you have an Enemy who has targeted you. Satan and his forces have studied you, and they have a plan already in motion through which they are determined to break you down, gobble you up, and spit out the pieces.

After all, this is the nature of villains. It's what they do. Emperor Palpatine in the *Star Wars* saga didn't have a mild disagreement with the Rebellion. He wanted to grind up every ship and every soul who dared to defy him. Lord Voldemort in the *Harry Potter* series wasn't interested in treaties with Harry. He wanted "the boy who lived" to be the boy who died. Thanos in the *Avengers* movies wasn't trying to make a better universe (though he said that all the time). He was trying to impose his will on the universe, even at the cost of trillions of lives.

The villain in our story is likewise interested in crushing us. However, as the apostle Paul wrote, "we are not unaware of his schemes" (2 Corinthians 2:11). We know the Enemy's strategies. We can boil his plans down to six specific methods of attack: deception, destruction, distraction, disunity, deconstruction, and desensitization. This week, we will look at his strategies of destruction and distraction and see how the spiritual armor we discussed in this session—the belt of truth and breastplate of righteousness—can help us fend off his attacks.

1. *How would the Enemy take you out?* **Think about that question—about the** specific steps Satan is likely to take in order to attack you and attempt to destroy you. Use the boxes below to write down what comes to mind.

What are some vulnerabilities that Satan could seek to exploit in your life?

What are some areas of pride or vanity that Satan could seek to inflame?

What are some other areas of weakness that Satan could try to infiltrate?

---

2. Think back to a season of your life when the Enemy was successful in harming you or knocking you off the path of righteousness. What did you learn during that time? What mistakes did you make that you can avoid in the future?

Recently I read about a biosphere where a group of scientists had created a perfect environment to grow certain plants and trees. One thing they found was that the trees in this environment—complete with the perfect soil, amount of sunlight, and watering—grew up at a rapid pace. But then they fell over. They set out to discover why that happened, and I thought their conclusion was fascinating. Why did they topple over? There was no wind in the biosphere and so the trees were never tested. Their root systems were not strengthened in the soil. There were no deep roots, so at the slightest hint of adversity they collapsed.

So many of us have grown up in an environment where it was totally normal to carry a Bible, walk into a room, sing songs, walk out, go get Mexican food afterward, and talk about whether or not we liked the sermon or the worship setlist. Then when the Enemy comes after you, you wonder why you fall over like a tree with no roots. I have seen this in my own life and in the lives of people I love and care about.[13]

3. When have you been tested or made to endure attacks in a way that produced strength? What are some tests you are facing now, and where are you in danger of toppling?

4. Look again at the six patterns of attack often used by Satan: deception, destruction, distraction, disunity, deconstruction, and desensitization. Where do you see one or more of those attacks at work in your community right now? Your family? Your church?

[8]Be alert and of sober mind. Your enemy the devil prowls around like a roaring lion looking for someone to devour. [9]Resist him, standing firm in the faith, because you know that the family of believers throughout the world is undergoing the same kind of sufferings. [10]And the God of all grace, who called you to his eternal glory in Christ, after you have suffered a little while, will himself restore you and make you strong, firm and steadfast. [11]To him be the power for ever and ever. Amen (1 Peter 5:8–11).

5. As you think back on your life, what has been helpful in resisting Satan so far? What have you tried that was successful at resisting him? What have you tried that was not successful?

THE VILLAIN DECEIVES

The more we ponder Satan and his demons and their involvement in our lives, the more questions come to mind. Despite the church existing for two millennia, there is still quite a bit we don't know about the villain in our stories.

For example, how do Satan and his demonic forces communicate with us? How do they "speak" with (or speak at) regular human beings like us? Like angels, demons are spiritual beings. They can interact with our world, and we know from the Bible that they can sometimes even manifest themselves in ways that we can see, hear, or even touch. Think of Adam and Eve in the garden of Eden. Think of Satan tempting Jesus in the wilderness. Think of "Legion" speaking with Jesus before being sent into the herd of pigs.

Demons can connect with our plane of existence, but they primarily live and operate in the spiritual plane. So, how do they talk to us? How do they tempt us? How do they push us toward what is dangerous and destructive? Thinking of Satan specifically, how does he communicate his lies and his deception? Is it some kind of telepathy? As spiritual beings, do Satan and his forces whisper to our spirits in ways that are beyond human perception?

We don't know. The Bible doesn't offer clarity about the function or the method for Satan's communication with humanity. However, what the Bible does make clear is that Satan is a liar. He is a deceiver. Whenever he speaks or communicates or in any way transmits his will to our will, he does so in ways that are deceitful. As John said of him, he is "that ancient serpent called the devil, or Satan, who leads the whole world astray" (Revelation 12:9).

Note that there is a difference between lies and deception. Both are dangerous, of course, but there is a sense in which we can identify a liar and make him or her less dangerous. When we know someone is a liar, we don't believe that person. However, someone who is deceptive is different. Such a person makes us *believe* that he or she is telling the truth. This is the tactic Satan has used and again and again for thousands of years—which is why it is so important for us to put on the *belt of truth* so we can see through his schemes.

1. How good are you at discerning whether or not people are lying to you? Consider the following categories and note your response.

How good are you at telling when people are lying about facts, data, evidence, and other types of information?

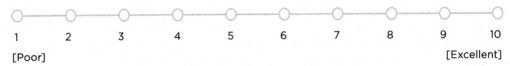

1   2   3   4   5   6   7   8   9   10

[Poor]   [Excellent]

How good are you at telling when people are lying about themselves—about their character, their personality, their history, and so on?

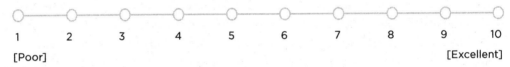

1   2   3   4   5   6   7   8   9   10

[Poor]   [Excellent]

How good are you at telling when people are deceiving or manipulating you in order to benefit themselves? (When people are using you?)

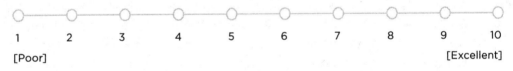

1   2   3   4   5   6   7   8   9   10

[Poor]   [Excellent]

2. Jesus taught, "Watch out for false prophets. They come to you in sheep's clothing, but inwardly they are ferocious wolves. By their fruit you will recognize them" (Matthew 7:15–16). What "fruit" do false teachers produce? How does putting on the belt of truth enable you to recognize a false teacher by the kind of "fruit" that he or she produces?

12 And I will keep on doing what I am doing in order to cut the ground from under those who want an opportunity to be considered equal with us in the things they boast about. 13 For such people are false apostles, deceitful workers, masquerading as apostles of Christ. 14 And no wonder, for Satan himself masquerades as an angel of light. 15 It is not surprising, then, if his servants also masquerade as servants of righteousness. Their end will be what their actions deserve (2 Corinthians 11:12–15).

3. Paul paints an ominous picture in these verses—not just of Satan appearing as an angel of light but also of false teachers appearing as "servants of righteousness." How do you think Paul could recognize these teachers (with their fine-sounding arguments) as the false teachers they actually were? How can knowing God's Word (the belt of truth) likewise protect you from false doctrines and those who proclaim them?

[Satan] and his forces cannot read your mind in a traditional sense. . . . But here is a disclaimer: I *do* believe he can read your mind in a different sense. Here is an example: Sometimes when I am talking with Monica, I'll say, "How do you feel about this situation?" She'll say, "I don't know how I feel right now." Then I'll say, "Well, it seems like you feel this, this, this, and this." And she'll say, "That is *exactly* how I feel. I just was unable to put it in words."

Why can I do that? Because I have studied her. I have committed to understanding how her mind works. In the same way, Satan (or some demon) has studied you and understands how you think, what trips you up, what will take you out. He did it with your great-great-great-grandparent. He's been lying to generations of your family. His angels know where you're vulnerable, what you like, and what makes you very angry. They cannot force the believer to think something, but they can lie to you. They can influence your thoughts, and this is why the truth is so important.[14]

4. Demons have been around for thousands of years, so there is a good chance that these spiritual enemies have been connected with your family for generations. Use the space below to record some of the main struggles, addictions, patterns of sin, and other attacks that you feel might be present (or have been present) in your extended family.

> What are some ways your grandparents might have been attacked spiritually?

> What are some ways your parents might have been attacked spiritually?

> What are some ways your siblings might have been attacked spiritually?

> If you have children, in what ways might the Enemy have attacked them spiritually?

5. What are some of the patterns of attack that the Enemy has used against your family as a whole? Where do you see those attacks present in your own life?

THE VILLAIN DESTROYS

There aren't many phenomena in the natural world more destructive than a tornado. You've likely seen some of those videos from security cameras mounted to schools or homes that show what happens when a tornado comes screaming by. It's crazy!

First, the wind starts to howl and spin. You can see trees swooping from left to right, then right to left, like they're trying to learn a new dance. The sky turns the color of dark purple, sometimes tinged with a sickly green. Then you see debris start to swirl around—pieces of trash, twigs, leaves, bags, yard signs, and more. The rain pours down in sheets and lightning snaps in the background. Then, just when the actual funnel cloud comes into the frame of the camera, you stop seeing debris swirling in the wind and start to see actual stuff. Like trash cans and trampolines and shingles and whole bushes plucked out of the ground.

Finally, just when you think the building you are seeing in the shot is going to survive . . . a wall breaks. Or the roof caves in at a certain spot. Or a door gets ripped off its hinges. At that point, it seems like all hell breaks loose. The whole building disintegrates into a pile of rubble, while parts of it continue to be whipped around and tossed upward into the sky.

If left unchecked, this is the kind of force that Satan would use to rip through our lives every single day. What he seeks to accomplish in our lives at every possible moment can only be described as complete destruction and utter chaos. However, thankfully, Satan has never been left unchecked. In spite of all his rage, hatred, and destructive potential, he remains locked under the sovereignty of God, just like every other created thing.

Now, this can raise some potentially troubling questions, and we're going to explore several of those together in the pages to come. But for now, focus on one important truth: *Satan is far more destructive than a tornado but is also on a short leash*. He remains under the direct authority and control of God. So, when you encounter a season of destruction, you can put on the armor of God and trust that He will help you see it through to the end.

1. Where do you see evidence today that Satan has immense destructive power? Where do you see evidence that his power is under God's control?

³ Then the Lᴏʀᴅ said to Satan, "Have you considered my servant Job? There is no one on earth like him; he is blameless and upright, a man who fears God and shuns evil. And he still maintains his integrity, though you incited me against him to ruin him without any reason."

⁴ "Skin for skin!" Satan replied. "A man will give all he has for his own life. ⁵ But now stretch out your hand and strike his flesh and bones, and he will surely curse you to your face."

⁶ The Lᴏʀᴅ said to Satan, "Very well, then, he is in your hands; but you must spare his life."

⁷ So Satan went out from the presence of the Lᴏʀᴅ and afflicted Job with painful sores from the soles of his feet to the crown of his head. ⁸ Then Job took a piece of broken pottery and scraped himself with it as he sat among the ashes.

⁹ His wife said to him, "Are you still maintaining your integrity? Curse God and die!"

¹⁰ He replied, "You are talking like a foolish woman. Shall we accept good from God, and not trouble?"

In all this, Job did not sin in what he said (Job 2:3–10).

2. The story of Job gives us a unique glimpse into the spiritual world. In the passage above, underline what God says about Job that indicates he was leading a righteous life. What does this tell us about a person who is truly putting on the breastplate of righteousness?

3. Notice that Satan's desire was to *destroy* Job and that he actually took steps to destroy him (within the parameters set by God). Take a look at how Job's wife responds when Satan does (see verse 9). What lie of the Enemy is she believing in that moment? How does Job demonstrate that he understands the *truth* about God (see verse 10)?

Each one of these moments [of trial]—when the disaster strikes, when the loss happens, when the diagnosis is given—presents us with the opportunity to either trust God or not. Think about it this way: if life were exclusively rainbows and butterflies, you would not need faith. The biggest thing God wants from you is faith. He wants you to trust Him. And each one of these moments is an opportunity for you to grow your faith.[15]

4. Read James 1:2–4. A common tactic of the Enemy is to first cause destruction in your life and then try to get you to believe that God would have prevented it if He were truly loving and good. (This is why you need to make sure you are putting on the belt of truth and the breastplate of righteousness each day.) According to James, what purpose might those trials be serving other than the immediate discomfort you are feeling at having to endure them?

5. Every moment you encounter destruction is an opportunity to trust God with your circumstances—even when you don't understand why the Lord allowed that destruction in the first place. What obstacles have prevented you from trusting God in the past?

CATCH UP AND READ AHEAD

Take time today to connect with a group member and talk about some of the insights from this session. Use any of the prompts below to help guide your discussion.

- What ideas felt confusing from this session, including both the group study and personal study? What questions would you like to have answered?
- What is something new you learned this week about Satan?
- Every time you encounter destruction is an opportunity to lean into God and trust Him. Where do you have an opportunity to trust God right now?
- Satan employs methods not only of destruction but also of deception. Are you confident in your ability to discern when someone is trying to deceive you? Why or why not?
- What practical ways could you equip the belt of truth and the breastplate of righteousness this week? How would you benefit if you did this?

Use this time to go back and complete any of the study and reflection questions from previous days that you weren't able to finish. Make a note below of any revelations you've had and reflect on any growth or personal insights you've gained.

Read chapters 5 and 7 in *Your Story Has a Villain* before the next group session. Use the space below to note anything that stands out to you or encourages you.

WEEK 3

BEFORE GROUP MEETING	Read chapters 5 and 7 in *Your Story Has a Villain* Read the Welcome section (page 46)
GROUP MEETING	Discuss the Connect questions Watch the video teaching for session 3 Discuss the questions that follow as a group Do the closing exercise and pray (pages 46–50)
STUDY 1	Complete the personal study (pages 53–56)
STUDY 2	Complete the personal study (pages 57–60)
STUDY 3	Complete the personal study (pages 61–64)
CATCH UP AND READ AHEAD (BEFORE WEEK 4 GROUP MEETING)	Connect with someone in your group Read chapters 8–9 in *Your Story Has a Villain* Complete any unfinished personal studies (page 65)

HOLD FIRM TO THE GOSPEL AND TO FAITH

[Stand firm] with your feet fitted with the readiness that comes from the gospel of peace. In addition to all this, take up the shield of faith, with which you can extinguish all the flaming arrows of the evil one.

EPHESIANS 6:15-16

WELCOME | READ ON YOUR OWN

Did you know that exoskeleton suits are a thing? We're not talking science fiction here. We're not talking about anything you've seen in the movies or in TV shows. We're talking real life. Right this very moment, you can hop online and order yourself a hydraulic exoskeleton suit to help you lift stuff, move stuff, or just generally be awesome.[16]

Admittedly, these exoskeleton suits are not the same as what Ridley used to fight the xenomorph in the *Alien* movies. At least, not yet. Modern exoskeleton suits look more like a type of thin scaffolding that you strap around your arms, legs, and back. Actually, they kind of look like a fancy set of metallic suspenders. And, yes, those suits are mostly being developed for use by the military and, in some cases, by warehouse workers and those who need to lift things for a living. So, the tech hasn't yet completely hit the mainstream. But still . . . we're talking about opening the door to superhuman strength! This is Tony Stark–level stuff!

Speaking of superhuman strength, in the previous session we introduced two super-natural pieces of armor that God uses to equip His saints: the belt of truth and the breastplate of righteousness. We are going to continue exploring the armor of God in this session. Specifically, we are going to look at having our feet "fitted with the readiness that comes from the gospel of peace" and at the "shield of faith," with which we can "extinguish all the flaming arrows of the evil one" (Ephesians 6:15–16).

Both of those pieces of the armor of God will be critical as we equip ourselves with a spiritual exoskeleton that will allow us to stand against the spiritual forces of evil in the heavenly realms.

CONNECT | 10 MINUTES

Get things started by discussing one of the following questions:

- What is something that resonated with you in last week's personal study that you would like to share with the group?

  — or —

- How would you summarize or describe the concept of "the gospel"?

WATCH | 25 MINUTES

Now watch the video for this session. Below is an outline of the key points covered during the teaching. Record any key concepts that stand out to you.

OUTLINE

I. We are called to stand against Satan's attacks by donning the next two pieces of spiritual armor:
- A. "Feet fitted with . . . the *gospel of peace*" (Ephesians 6:15).
- B. "The *shield of faith*, with which you can extinguish all the flaming arrows" (Ephesians 6:16).

II. Remember that Paul wrote Ephesians while he was a prisoner of Rome.
- A. Paul was likely chained to a soldier while he was imprisoned (c. AD 60–62).
- B. Paul drew on the Roman armor that he saw each day to describe the believer's spiritual armor.

III. We often think of faith as a spiritual fire extinguisher—something to use in case of emergency.
- A. *Faith* means to trust in God, but often what we do is pray we won't need faith.
- B. We tend to pray for things to rely on other than faith: resources, relationships, trinkets, and treasures. *Anything* that will allow us not to need to use our faith.
- C. True faith begins with us believing the gospel (see Ephesians 2:8–9).

IV. The shoes of the gospel of peace remind us that the *gospel* is the foundation of everything we do.
- A. The gospel is the "good news" that Christ became flesh so that we could be saved.
- B. The gospel is a source of peace in our lives. One of our biggest fears in this life is the reality that one day we will die. However, the gospel assures us that we have eternal life.
- C. We often need to adjust what we believe—even remove old traditions or habits that have become harmful. Everything must be built on the foundation of faith.

V. The shield of faith helps us to extinguish the *fiery darts* of Satan.
- A. These fiery darts are discouragement. Satan literally wants to *dis*-courage us by removing our courage and our faith in God.
- B. Satan tries to convince us that God is not good, that God does not really love us, and that God is not in control.
- C. We need to use the tools that God has given us to combat the Enemy.

NOTES

DISCUSS | 35 MINUTES

Now discuss what you just watched by answering the following questions.

1. Begin by discussing a few of the questions that were raised at the end of this week's teaching. What can you do to increase your faith? How can you renew your mind around the gospel regularly? When did you last share the gospel?

2. Paul states that believers in Christ are to have feet "fitted with the readiness that comes from the gospel of peace" (Ephesians 6:15). In your experience, what is the connection between the gospel and peace? How has the gospel personally brought you peace?

3. We are also to "take up the shield of faith" (Ephesians 6:16). *Faith* is a word that gets used a lot today, but often we don't examine what it really means or what it looks like in everyday life. How would you describe what faith is and what faith requires from us?

4. Ask someone to read aloud Matthew 6:24. Often, we try to bypass faith by praying for things that feel more secure to us—like relationships, status, and especially money. What warning does Jesus give in this verse about relying on the things of this world instead of on the things of God? What does it look like to trust God rather than our own resources?

5. Ask someone to read Mark 16:15. This week's teaching ended with an important question: *When was the last time you shared the gospel with someone?* If it's been a long time, what obstacles have hindered your ability or your willingness to share the gospel with others?

RESPOND | 10 MINUTES

Boiled down to its simplest definition, faith is trust in God. When we demonstrate faith, we actively trust God with all that we are and everything we have. The author of Hebrews helps us flesh that definition out a bit more and apply it to our spiritual lives:

> [1] Now faith is confidence in what we hope for and assurance about what we do not see. [2] This is what the ancients were commended for. [3] By faith we understand that the universe was formed at God's command, so that what is seen was not made out of what was visible. . . . [5] By faith Enoch was taken from this life, so that he did not experience death: "He could not be found, because God had taken him away." For before he was taken, he was commended as one who pleased God. [6] And without faith it is impossible to please God, because anyone who comes to him must believe that he exists and that he rewards those who earnestly seek him.
>
> **HEBREWS 11:1–3, 5–6**

How is faith defined in this passage? How can we balance the need for faith in our spiritual lives with our desire to know God's will and have our questions answered?

The author of Hebrews writes, "Without faith it is impossible to please God" (verse 6). When have you done something that you sincerely believe pleased God? How was faith involved in that moment or that season?

PRAY | 10 MINUTES

Conclude this session by expressing your desire to be equipped with each piece of the armor of God, including having your feet fitted with the readiness that comes from the gospel of peace and taking up the shield of faith. Ask that God would help you to deflect the fiery darts that the Enemy sends your way and that He would fill each person in your group with His peace. Finally, ask that each of you would see every opportunity available to please God through faith.

PERSONAL STUDY

When it comes to the villain in your story, it is important not only to know about the spiritual armor God has made available to you but also to know what schemes the Enemy will employ against you. In the previous session, we discussed how Satan will use deception and destruction to derail you and how you can put on the belt of truth and the breastplate of righteousness to weather those attacks. In this week's personal study, you will examine how the Enemy uses distraction and disunity as a weapon and how the shield of faith and the shoes of the gospel can equip you to stand strong against those attacks. As you work through these exercises, continue to write down your responses to the questions, as you will be given a few minutes to share your insights and key takeaways at the start of the next session. If you are reading *Your Story Has a Villain* alongside this study, first review chapters 5 and 7 in the book.

For it is by grace you have been saved, through faith.

EPHESIANS 2:8

SATAN AS ACCUSER

Let's return to the story of Job. One thing that we might find surprising is that Satan plays a relatively minor role in Job's story in terms of what we might call his "screen time." He shows up for only the first two chapters of a forty-two-chapter book. However, whenever Satan does show up, he functions as an accuser.

At the beginning of the story, Satan appears before the Lord when the angels come to present themselves in heaven (which is an interesting idea on its own). When God brings up Job as an example of a righteous and faithful servant in His kingdom, Satan responds with accusations: "Have you not put a hedge around him and his household and everything he has? You have blessed the work of his hands, so that his flocks and herds are spread throughout the land. But now stretch out your hand and strike everything he has, and he will surely curse you to your face" (Job 1:10–11).

In the next chapter of Job, God again tells Satan to consider His servant's faithfulness even in the midst of his suffering. Once again, Satan responds by accusing Job of only holding on to his faith because God had kept him physically healthy: "Skin for skin! . . . A man will give all he has for his own life. But now stretch out your hand and strike his flesh and bones, and he will surely curse you to your face" (2:4–5).

This isn't an isolated incident. Throughout the Bible, Satan is identified as an accuser. For reasons difficult to understand, that is part of his role in the universe. He constantly brings accusations against the members of God's kingdom. Often, these accusations are internal: the Enemy accuses us to *us*. It's like he's hovering behind us, whispering accusations into our minds: "You are such a poor provider for your family. Here you are craving a cigarette again; you are never going to break through this addiction. Your whole life is meaningless right now, and nothing you've done will amount to anything." Accusation after accusation. All designed to bring us down.

At other times, Satan will use other people to accuse us. He manipulates them to speak falsely against us or accuse us of wrongdoing. Again, Satan's ultimate goal in doing this is *deception* and *destruction*—and again, the way that we successfully counter these attacks is by putting on the armor of God.

1. Use the circle on the left to write down the accusations you hear internally on a regular basis—things that feel like failures or defects that often come to mind. Use the right circle to make a list of positive things you know to be true about yourself—positive elements of your character and behavior.

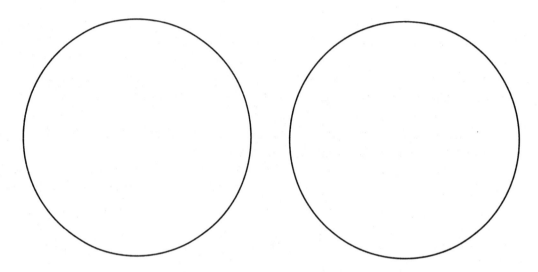

2. One of the ways we can see the accuser at work is the incredibly high prevalence of anxiety, depression, and suicidal thoughts in our society today. People are more anxious and depressed than ever, and that is at least partly because we are listening more than ever to Satan's accusations. How does our culture teach us to deal with those negative thoughts?

This is the reason so many Christians live lives of isolation, shame, and guilt. The Enemy *loves* when we keep our mess in the dark. The accuser *loves* for you to feel like you are the only one struggling with a certain sin, and that you cannot or should not tell people about it. Some of you reading this right now have things in your past (or even right now) that you think you're going to take to the grave. You say, "That's an aspect of my life I'm going to continue to hide from people because if they knew that thing about me, they would reject me." Some of the usual suspects are abortion, abuse, addiction, and sexual perversion or desires.

I understand the desire to keep that a secret because I *was* that person as I sat on the back row in a church with a pounding headache from a night of partying. I was thinking, *These people in their Sunday best, they can't relate to me!* And that is right where the Enemy wants us to stay forever and ever—with secrets. The Scriptures call us to walk in the light and be children of the light (1 John 1:7-9) and to confess our sins to one another and be healed (James 5:16). Whenever we feel tempted to keep "that thing" in the dark, that's not of the Spirit. That's the accuser out to deceive us and pull us away from the truth of the Scriptures.[17]

3. Read Acts 2:42–47. This passage describes the early church immediately after Peter preached his sermon on the Day of Pentecost that led to around 3,000 converts. Think about a typical week in your life. Out of seven days, how often do you experience a meaningful form of community like this—fellowship, sharing, prayer, and interaction with people you care about? How often do you experience longer periods of being alone?

4. Sharing with others about our struggles is always difficult—but it's also necessary for spiritual health. Who can you speak honestly with about your sins and mistakes? Who helps you to put on the armor of God each and every day?

[14] But as for you, continue in what you have learned and have become convinced of, because you know those from whom you learned it, [15] and how from infancy you have known the Holy Scriptures, which are able to make you wise for salvation through faith in Christ Jesus. [16] All Scripture is God-breathed and is useful for teaching, rebuking, correcting and training in righteousness, [17] so that the servant of God may be thoroughly equipped for every good work (2 Timothy 3:14–17).

5. Think about what you learned this week concerning the shield of faith and the shoes of the gospel of peace. How does the shield of faith enable you to deflect Satan's fiery arrows of anxiety and discouragement? How do the shoes of the gospel of peace provide you with the assurance of your salvation so that you can experience God's perfect peace?

THE VILLAIN DISTRACTS

There are many examples of famous last words in history. For instance, Sir Isaac Newton was a well-known mathematician, but his last words were both theological and philosophical: "I don't know what I may seem to the world. But as to myself I seem to have been only like a boy playing on the seashore and diverting myself now and then in finding a smoother pebble or a prettier shell than the ordinary, whilst the great ocean of truth lay all undiscovered before me."

Others were more practical with their last words. As Benjamin Franklin lay on his deathbed, his daughter asked him to shift positions so he could breathe more easily. "A dying man can do nothing easy," the statesman said. Then he died.

Still others gave voice to their final words in ways that were memorable to those who were near them. Arthur Conan Doyle, the author who is famous for creating Sherlock Holmes, turned to his wife and exclaimed, "You are wonderful," before clutching his chest. Legendary football coach Vince Lombardi's final statement was also given to his wife: "Happy anniversary; I love you." And Apple founder Steve Jobs was talking to his sister, Mona, when he uttered his final words: "Oh wow. Oh wow. Oh wow."[18]

The Bible records Jesus' last words—although those words were delivered not at the moment of His death but prior to His return to heaven. Standing on a mountain in Galilee with the disciples, He told them, "All authority in heaven and on earth has been given to me. Therefore go and make disciples of all nations, baptizing them in the name of the Father and of the Son and of the Holy Spirit, and teaching them to obey everything I have commanded you. And surely I am with you always, to the very end of the age" (Matthew 28:18–20).

These words describe our *mission* as followers of Jesus. They are the base command we are called to follow—to go and make disciples in Jesus' name. For that reason, we can be sure that the Enemy will do everything possible to prevent us from undertaking that mission. He will tell us lies, try to make this important mission God has given us look cheap, and seek to distract us. However, we can deflect these attacks if we put on the armor of God.

1. How easily do you get distracted in the following situations?

When you're trying to study or read something:

1   2   3   4   5   6   7   8   9   10

[Almost never]   [Frequently]

When you're at work:

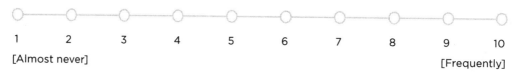

1   2   3   4   5   6   7   8   9   10

[Almost never]   [Frequently]

When you're driving:

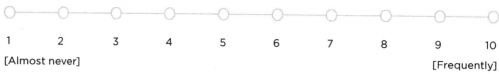

1   2   3   4   5   6   7   8   9   10

[Almost never]   [Frequently]

2. The instruction that Jesus gave to His followers to "go and make disciples" is critical because it could be the only means through which people learn about salvation in Christ. You could literally be the one who saves another person from an eternity in hell because they heard about the gospel through *you.* Clearly, this mission is valuable. But what are some of the ways the Enemy tries to cheapen it? How have you personally witnessed the Enemy try to distract you and other followers of Christ from living out this mission to the world?

You're not just distracted. You are being distracted strategically by the one who seeks to keep you from the pleasures of God. He's dangling all the world has to offer in an effort to appeal to your worldly desires. And for so many people, he is incredibly successful. And what's at stake here? Honestly, the future of the world. Jesus' commission compels us to go and make disciples. One reason we don't do this is that we are so distracted with our lives, our classes, our work, our families, and our conflicts. We—and I'm talking about the church (particularly the Western church)—don't spend enough time focusing on the life of Jesus, so that we might emulate it for others.[19]

3. Satan is continually trying to distract you from the things of God—including your mission to go and make disciples. This is why it is important to put on the shoes of the gospel of peace. You need to be sure that your life is built on the foundation of your faith in Christ and that you are sharing the message of the gospel with those who need to receive it. In the table below, list a few of the ways that Satan has distracted you when it comes to sharing your faith. Next to those items, list some ways you could counter those attacks.

Distractions in sharing the gospel	How you could counter this attack

4. Satan will also distract you by using religion to make you think you're obeying Christ when actually you're just doing "church stuff." You're going through the motions without making an impact. How can you tell whether you are making a real difference for God's kingdom?

> 25 Let your eyes look straight ahead;
>   fix your gaze directly before you.
> 26 Give careful thought to the paths for your feet
>   and be steadfast in all your ways.
> 27 Do not turn to the right or the left;
>   keep your foot from evil (Proverbs 4:25–27)

5. Satan wants to distract you this week. He wants to distract you from pursuing your faith in Christ. He wants to distract you from pursuing God's righteousness. He wants to distract you from sharing the gospel with others. What does it mean to "let your eyes look straight ahead" and "be steadfast in all your ways" when it comes to combating these distractions? What happens when you choose to be faithful and stick to God's path?

THE VILLAIN DISUNIFIES

It doesn't take a rocket scientist to recognize that most societies today are filled with divisions. In fact, it wouldn't be inaccurate to say most of our modern societies are *built* on divisions. In the United States, for example, there is a two-party political system that influences just about everything its citizens experience. Wouldn't you know it? About half the country thinks one party is right about most things, while the other half thinks the other party is right about most things. The country is pretty much split down the middle on a whole host of issues.

But here is the thing about such systems: When there are only two options on the table, it is natural for each side to criticize the other. We see this all the time today. Many politicians, instead of focusing on the qualities they have that make them a *good* choice for the job, will instead talk about why their opponents are a *bad* choice for the job. It is a strategy that has been popularized in so-called "attack ads," where one candidate seeks to discredit the other.

Sadly, political systems like those in the United States have endured decades of this kind of negativity, with the end result that the nation feels pulled apart at the seams.

But it's not just politics. Think about the way that generations are encouraged to squabble and find fault with one another. Or the way that parents are often put at odds with the education system. Or the level of hostility that viewers carry toward the media and news organizations. Or the adversarial relationship that exists between corporations and communities and between employers and employees. Think about the damage and the prevalence of divorce.

This constant division and disunity is not happening by accident. No, it is one of the Enemy's core strategies. He loves to pull things apart. And he especially loves to pull things apart when God brought them together. As we will see in this study, the church is supposed to be a counterculture to all the division and disunity in our world. The church is supposed to be unified in ways that transcend the squabbling and bickering and partisanship that makes up so much of our lives. That's our goal. That's our mission. But we can't do it on our own.

1. Using the following scale, to what degree do you experience division and dis-unity in the following spheres of life?

At home (within your family):

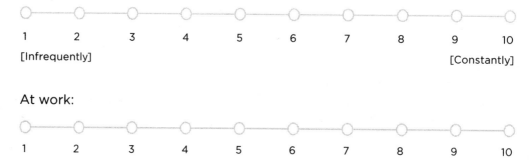

1   2   3   4   5   6   7   8   9   10

[Infrequently]   [Constantly]

At work:

1   2   3   4   5   6   7   8   9   10

[Infrequently]   [Constantly]

Within your neighborhood or community:

1   2   3   4   5   6   7   8   9   10

[Infrequently]   [Constantly]

Within your church:

1   2   3   4   5   6   7   8   9   10

[Infrequently]   [Constantly]

2. Disunity is one of Satan's core strategies—and it is a strategy that he has been using for a *loooooooooong* time. (There's really nothing new when it comes to his tactics.) This is evidenced by the fact that disunity reared its ugly head even during the early days of the church. In the passage below, in which Paul is discussing the different factions that have broken out in Corinth, underline or circle all the places where you see signs of disunity.

> [10] I appeal to you, brothers and sisters, in the name of our Lord Jesus Christ, that all of you agree with one another in what you say and that there be no

divisions among you, but that you be perfectly united in mind and thought. [11] My brothers and sisters, some from Chloe's household have informed me that there are quarrels among you. [12] What I mean is this: One of you says, "I follow Paul"; another, "I follow Apollos"; another, "I follow Cephas"; still another, "I follow Christ."

[13] Is Christ divided? Was Paul crucified for you? Were you baptized in the name of Paul? [14] I thank God that I did not baptize any of you except Crispus and Gaius, [15] so no one can say that you were baptized in my name. [16] (Yes, I also baptized the household of Stephanas; beyond that, I don't remember if I baptized anyone else.) [17] For Christ did not send me to baptize, but to preach the gospel—not with wisdom and eloquence, lest the cross of Christ be emptied of its power (1 Corinthians 1:10–17).

Take a look at the words or phrases that you highlighted in this passage. What does this say about what was going on in the church in Corinth? Where do you see signs that the Enemy is using this same tactic today—by causing different factions to break out in the church?

3. Read Hebrews 10:23–25. Recall from this week's group time that the shoes of the gospel of peace enable you to know that your faith is built on a solid foundation while the shield of faith allows you to stand strong on that foundation and deflect the Enemy's attacks. How does belonging to a church where the gospel is preached help you to put on the shoes? How does belonging to a group of believers who have weathered trials in their lives help you to put on the shield? Why is it so important to "not [give] up meeting together"?

Unity is an apologetic—a defense of our faith—to a world that is so easily divided. So if the world sees Christians whose bond in Jesus overrides politics and preferences, they say, "That Jesus guy must have been real. He must have come from the Father. There is no other reason those people would get along." I believe that message has been lost somewhere along the way, so that's why I want you to know explicitly that this is what Jesus prayed for you.

Do you realize that, by being a part of a Bible-teaching, healthy church, you have a bigger target on your back? If your church is dysfunctional and nobody gets along and everyone has their own agenda, that is playing right into the villain's hand. Satan is always after works of God. For some people, that freaks them out. They hear that and they want out, because they didn't mean to sign up for that. They're thinking, *Man, I don't want to be under attack. I don't want the Enemy to know who I am.* The alternative way is living a faithless life, full of indulging in your own pleasure.[20]

4. These days, people coming together in unity is often a surprising experience. Where do you see opportunities for the church to heal some of the divisions that are currently impacting our culture and world? What would it look like if followers of Jesus truly sought to be united in their mission of sharing the gospel and serving those in need—as the Bible instructs us to do?

5. Read James 4:7. Satan works to sow seeds of division in the church, but we are called to resist him and prevent those seeds from sprouting. So, what can you and your church do to foster unity in your community? How would this be an act of resisting the devil?

CATCH UP AND READ AHEAD

Take time today to connect with a group member and talk about some of the insights from this session. Use any of the prompts below to help guide your discussion.

- Which elements of this session caught your attention in a meaningful way? Why those particular elements?
- What does it look like (at a practical level) to resist Satan when he hurls his accusations against you?
- One tactic that Satan loves to employ—which is quite effective today—is distraction. Do you find it easy or difficult to get rid of what is unhealthy in your life when it comes to distractions? Explain.
- Unity in the church is powerful. It catches the world's attention. When have you seen the power of God's people working together as a united front?
- What are some practical ways you could equip the shoes of the gospel of peace and the shield of faith this week? What are some ways you will share the gospel with others?

Use this time to go back and complete any of the study and reflection questions from previous days that you weren't able to finish. Make a note below of any revelations you've had and reflect on any growth or personal insights you've gained.

Read chapters 8–9 in *Your Story Has a Villain* before the next group session. Use the space below to note anything that stands out to you or encourages you.

WEEK 4

BEFORE GROUP MEETING	Read chapters 8–9 in *Your Story Has a Villain* Read the Welcome section (page 68)
GROUP MEETING	Discuss the Connect questions Watch the video teaching for session 4 Discuss the questions that follow as a group Do the closing exercise and pray (pages 68–72)
STUDY 1	Complete the personal study (pages 75–78)
STUDY 2	Complete the personal study (pages 79–82)
STUDY 3	Complete the personal study (pages 83–86)
CATCH UP AND READ AHEAD (BEFORE WEEK 5 GROUP MEETING)	Connect with someone in your group Read chapters 10–13 in *Your Story Has a Villain* Complete any unfinished personal studies (page 87)

BE MINDFUL OF YOUR SALVATION AND GOD'S WORD

Take the helmet of salvation and the sword of the Spirit, which is the word of God.

EPHESIANS 6:17

WELCOME | READ ON YOUR OWN

The human brain is pretty incredible when you think about it. It is a marvelous organ that provides us with the capacity for thought, memory, reasoning, sensation, emotion, and more. Our brains are wonders of the natural world.

Scientists estimate that a typical human brain consists of approximately eighty-six billion neurons. Each one of those neurons forms complex links with its neighboring neurons, which means that our brains are intensely multifaceted networks powered by more than a quadrillion connections. Beyond that, information travels throughout the neurons, nerves, and synapses of our brains at about 350 miles per hour. Our brains are also extremely busy. Researchers believe the average person has between 12,000 and 60,000 separate thoughts every day.[21]

So, yes, the organ we call the brain is pretty amazing. What is especially incredible is that our brains somehow house what we think of as our "mind." Meaning, our ability to think and reason and feel on an emotional level. *Cogito ergo sum* . . . "I think, therefore I am." It's the mind that produces our sense of identity. Our consciousness. Our uniqueness.

Of course, Satan understands the immense value of our minds. He understands the potential of our ability to think—probably at a deeper level than we do. He covets our minds because he wants to limit our ability to use that resource as an asset within God's kingdom. He wants to capture our minds and turn them against us. Our Enemy is after our minds, and he plays for keeps. This is a reality. So, the question is, What are we going to do about it?

CONNECT | 10 MINUTES

Get things started by discussing one of the following questions:

- What is something that resonated with you in last week's personal study that you would like to share with the group?

  — *or* —

- What emotions do you experience when it comes to sharing your testimony? Why does sharing your story of salvation cause you to react that way?

WATCH | 25 MINUTES

Now watch the video for this session. Below is an outline of the key points covered during the teaching. Record any key concepts that stand out to you.

OUTLINE

I. We are called to stand against Satan's attacks by donning the next two pieces of spiritual armor:

   A. "Take the *helmet of salvation*" (Ephesians 6:17a).

   B. "[Take] the *sword of the Spirit*, which is the word of God" (Ephesians 6:17b).

II. So much of what happens in our head controls our entire body.

   A. Paul says that we need to be *mindful* of our salvation each and every day.

   B. We have to remember the battle that Jesus fought on our behalf to secure our salvation.

   C. When we build our lives on that truth, we are one step closer to defeating the villain in our story.

III. The helmet of salvation will enable us to protect our *minds*.

   A. Satan wants the "real estate" of our minds. He wants to keep us focused on this world and make us hungry for things that never satisfy.

   B. The helmet of salvation protects our thinking by helping us remember we are saved by grace. We remember that we will one day be with God in eternity.

   C. The Holy Spirit gives us a "heart of flesh" when we come into salvation.

IV. The simple reality that we are saved by grace is the beginning of finding victory against temptation.

   A. We only have access to salvation because Jesus died for our sins.

   B. When we accept this and recognize that we are going to have a glorious and eternal inheritance with Jesus, we do not allow the worries or the temptations of this world to derail us.

   C. We allow the Holy Spirit to transform us through the renewing of our minds (Romans 12:1–2).

V. The sword of the Spirit (the Bible) is our weapon against the Enemy.

   A. Everything else that Paul discusses is *defensive* gear, but the sword of the Spirit is an *offensive* weapon that we use to strike back at the Enemy.

   B. If we want to be victorious in battle, we need to *know* the Word of God.

   C. God is getting His children back through the work of His Son. We have a "ticket" into heaven only because of Jesus' sacrifice on the cross.

NOTES

DISCUSS | 35 MINUTES

Now discuss what you just watched by answering the following questions.

1. Begin by asking a few people in the group to share their testimony of how they found salvation in Christ. They can describe what their life was like *before* they encountered Jesus, what the actual *moment* they encountered Jesus was like for them, and what their life is like now *after* they have received the free gift of salvation from Christ.

2. Salvation is a key idea in this session. How would you describe the concept of salvation (in a spiritual sense) to someone who has never heard of it before?

3. Ask someone to read aloud Romans 12:2. How would you define "the pattern of this world"? How have you seen the Holy Spirit work in your life to transform you and give you a spiritual appetite for the things of God?

4. Now consider the question mentioned in this week's teaching about knowing God's Word. What passages of Scripture have been especially meaningful or helpful in your spiritual life? Which passages of Scripture do you use as weapons against the villain in your story?

5. Ask someone to read aloud Hebrews 4:12–13. How is the Word of God described in this passage? What can this "double-edged sword" do in your life if you choose to wield it properly?

RESPOND | 10 MINUTES

Most people have a vague idea how to use a sword—stick the pointy end at the bad guy. However, we wouldn't be much use in an actual sword fight without the proper training. In the same way, it is helpful for us to see examples of people who have used the "sword of the Spirit" well to fight against Satan—including Jesus Himself.

> [1] Jesus, full of the Holy Spirit, left the Jordan and was led by the Spirit into the wilderness, [2] where for forty days he was tempted by the devil. He ate nothing during those days, and at the end of them he was hungry.
>
> [3] The devil said to him, "If you are the Son of God, tell this stone to become bread."
>
> [4] Jesus answered, "It is written: 'Man shall not live on bread alone.'"
>
> [5] The devil led him up to a high place and showed him in an instant all the kingdoms of the world. [6] And he said to him, "I will give you all their authority and splendor; it has been given to me, and I can give it to anyone I want to. [7] If you worship me, it will all be yours."
>
> [8] Jesus answered, "It is written: 'Worship the Lord your God and serve him only.'"
>
> **LUKE 4:1–8**

How did Jesus use the Bible as a weapon? What can you learn from His technique?

How confident do you feel in wielding God's Word as a weapon? What would it take for you to have the same confidence in using Scripture that Jesus possessed?

PRAY | 10 MINUTES

Conclude by professing the truth about salvation: We are saved by grace through faith in Christ alone. Proclaim your belief in Jesus and your desire to protect your mind with the helmet of salvation—and claim that protection out loud! Also ask that the Holy Spirit would continue to help you resist Satan and be someone "who correctly handles the word of truth" (2 Timothy 2:15).

PERSONAL STUDY

We have now looked at each piece of spiritual armor that we are instructed to put on each day, including the belt of truth, breastplate of righteousness, shoes of the gospel of peace, shield of faith, and helmet of salvation. We have also seen that God has given us the sword of the Spirit to strike back at the Enemy. In this week's personal study, you will focus on how you can especially use the helmet of salvation and the sword of the Spirit to counter the Enemy's tactics of desensitization and deconstruction. As you work through these exercises, continue to write down your responses, as you will be given a few minutes to share your insights and key takeaways at the start of the next session. If you are reading *Your Story Has a Villain* alongside this study, first review chapters 8–9 in the book.

The grass withers and the flowers fall, but the word of our God endures forever.

ISAIAH 40:8

SEEKING A FOOTHOLD

Who are the greatest athletes of our time? People throw many names in response to that question: Michael Jordan, Serena Williams, Simone Biles, Tom Brady, Messi, Mia Hamm, to name a few. Each has a legitimate case to being the "greatest."

However, if you're into rock climbing, you might add another name to that list: Alex Honnold. He has been recognized as the GOAT of rock climbing for a long time now, but he became semi-famous in 2017 when he accomplished something no other climber had tried: free-soloing the rock face of El Capitan in Yosemite National Park.

Now, if you are *not* into rock climbing, you need to know two things to truly appreciate that last sentence. First, the term *free solo* means to climb a rock face without using any equipment. No ropes. No nets. No carabiners. No self-tapping handholds. No safety equipment of any kind.

Second, El Capitan is a granite wall that is almost 3,000 feet high. This means that Alex started from the ground and clambered his way up 3,000 feet of a sheer mountainside using only his fingers, his toes, and a single bag of chalk. One mistake would have literally cost him his life as he plunged to his death. Thankfully, he made it. His climb lasted a grueling three hours and fifty-six minutes, but he made it.

Why mention this? Because for those roughly four hours of climbing time, Alex was entirely focused on handholds and footholds. Sure, there are spots on El Capitan that provide an "easy" climb for folks like Alex—big cracks and crags of rock that can be grabbed without trouble. Yet there are other spots on the cliffside where trembling fingers scrape to grab rocky outcroppings that are as little as 1/8 of an inch wide.

For thousands of years now, our Enemy has been focused on his own version of handholds and footholds—not on rocks, of course, but in our lives. Satan and his demonic forces work furiously to pry open some small gap that they can use to penetrate our lives with sin. And when they grab hold of us, it can be very difficult for us to shake them loose. This is why we need to make sure that we have put on *each* piece of spiritual armor and that it is securely in place.

1. Think about this idea of the Enemy seeking to secure handholds and footholds in your life. What does this reveal about the need for you to be equally as focused on making sure there is nothing there for him to grasp? As you consider each item of spiritual armor that God has provided, are you routinely forgetting to put on any certain piece of equipment?

In pastoral ministry, I've walked alongside a number of people and families in crisis. . . . One thing I have learned over the years is that very, very, very seldom (I hesitate to say "never") does someone wreck their life overnight. Very rarely do people wake up one morning and say, "Today is the day I want to throw it all away." They get there gradually as one pet sin turns into another pet sin, which then turns into even more sin.

In Ephesians 4:27, Paul said that we are not to give the devil even a foothold. Every time you sin, you are cracking the door open for the Enemy to come in. When you follow that hashtag, go to that website, say those words, hang out with those people, drink that stuff, smoke that thing—whatever your thing is—when you cross that line of what is holy and God-honoring, you crack the door and invite the Enemy into your life. Each time you give in to temptation, the door opens wider and wider, making it that much harder to kick the Enemy back out. This is *key* to understanding spiritual warfare.[22]

2. Read Ephesians 4:25–27. Paul states in this passage that you are not to "give the devil a foothold," which means any exposed area in your life that Satan can grab and use to start prying you away from God. What is the danger of allowing the Enemy to gain such a foothold?

3. It's easy to speak generally about sin and footholds—to talk about what "most people" struggle with in their lives. However, there comes a point when you need to identify your own "thing." So, where is Satan currently pressing against a crack in your life? Where does he have a foothold and is pushing you toward sin? List anything that comes to mind.

Where Satan is pressing against a crack	Where Satan is pushing me toward sin

> 8 If we claim to be without sin, we deceive ourselves and the truth is not in us. 9 If we confess our sins, he is faithful and just and will forgive us our sins and purify us from all unrighteousness (1 John 1:8–9).
>
> 14 If my people, who are called by my name, will humble themselves and pray and seek my face and turn from their wicked ways, then I will hear from heaven, and I will forgive their sin and will heal their land (2 Chronicles 7:14).

4. Confession and repentance are two critical steps we must take when removing the Enemy's footholds from our lives. *Confession* can be defined as the admission of sin. *Repentance* can be defined as a turning away from sin. Why are both necessary when it comes to removing strongholds? What is God's promise when we confess our sins and repent of them?

5. Read James 5:13–16. Community is another critical element when it comes to removing Satan's influence and footholds from our lives. How do you feel about speaking openly with others regarding the reality of sin? Who is one person in your life who can help you close the door to sin?

THE VILLAIN DECONSTRUCTS

The year 2020 was a wild time on this planet. Do we need to even say why? We've all heard enough about a certain virus that caused a lot of harm to so many people on earth. But 2020 was an important year for another reason, because something happened that year that had *never* happened before. Well . . . at least it had never happened before in the history of a country called the United States.

We are talking about church membership. In 2020, fewer than 50 percent of Americans identified themselves as members of a house of worship.[23] This means that less than half of all U.S. citizens even *claimed* to belong to a church, which is different even than measuring how many people actually left their homes and went to a house of worship during a given weekend. Less than half!

Church members are now a minority class in the United States. Can you believe that? Probably, you can. There has been a lot of attention in recent decades about the decline of faith in America. The number of people who believe in God and are serious about their faith has been trending down for years. Meanwhile, the number of people who identify as atheists or who simply don't care about faith has been rising sharply.

There are a lot of reasons for this decline, and you likely have your opinions about why this is taking place. However, one conclusion is that this new problem is the result of an old tactic that Satan has been using as a way to separate people from God. We can use the word *deconstruction* when we talk about this tactic because Satan's ultimate goal is to destroy our faith in the same way a construction crew might demolish a house at the beginning of a rehab project. How does Satan carry out that demolition? He gets us to question our faith by casting doubt on God—by questioning God's goodness, character, power, trustworthiness, involvement in our lives, and more.

It's the same old trick that he used all the way back in the garden of Eden with Adam and Eve. And how do we combat this type of attack? By taking up the helmet of salvation and making sure it is fitted securely to our head. We remember the *truth* that God has revealed to us in His Word and the battle Jesus fought on our behalf to secure our salvation. As we do this, we counter the Enemy's lies.

1. How have you witnessed changes in people's view of faith? Write down how people described Christians during the following time spans:

How did people view Christians and Christianity when you were growing up?

How did people view Christians and Christianity in your teenage years?

How did people view Christians and Christianity five years ago?

How do you see people viewing Christians and Christianity today?

2. Various studies show that faith and church attendance in the United States is on the decline. In places like Western Europe, it has been on the decline for quite some time. In fact, one study reports that Western Europe, where Protestant Christianity originated, "has become one of the world's most secular regions," with around only 22 percent of people attending church services on a monthly basis.[24] In your opinion, what are some root causes of this decline? What does this reveal about Satan's tactic of deconstruction?

> [1] Now the serpent was more crafty than any of the wild animals the LORD God had made. He said to the woman, "Did God really say, 'You must not eat from any tree in the garden'?"
>
> [2] The woman said to the serpent, "We may eat fruit from the trees in the garden, [3] but God did say, 'You must not eat fruit from the tree that is in the middle of the garden, and you must not touch it, or you will die.'"
>
> [4] "You will not certainly die," the serpent said to the woman. [5] "For God knows that when you eat from it your eyes will be opened, and you will be like God, knowing good and evil."
>
> [6] When the woman saw that the fruit of the tree was good for food and pleasing to the eye, and also desirable for gaining wisdom, she took some and ate it. She also gave some to her husband, who was with her, and he ate it. [7] Then the eyes of both of them were opened, and they realized they were naked; so they sewed fig leaves together and made coverings for themselves (Genesis 3:1–7).

3. Underline all the words spoken by the serpent to Adam and Eve. What strategies did Satan use to cast doubt on God's nature and character?

4. Remember from this week's teaching that all wars are fought over real estate. In your case, Satan wants the "real estate" of your mind. When has Satan tried to make you think that God does not have your best interests in mind? How does putting on the helmet of salvation every day help to protect you from such attacks of the Enemy?

When someone says, "I don't know what I believe anymore," my answer is always the same. I say, "Tell me, what do you believe about Jesus? Let's start there. Who is He?" We can get to the age of the earth later. We can get to dinosaurs. We can get to secondary and tertiary theological topics. Tell me what you believe about Jesus. The reason the disciples were able to reconstruct, after all they had been through, is that they had encountered Jesus. They had a whole new cornerstone to rebuild on top of.[25]

5. Read Philippians 2:12–13. In this passage, Paul advises you to "work out your salvation," which means donning the helmet of salvation and working out what you really believe about Jesus. So do this exercise right now. In the space below, write down a few statements about Jesus that you fully believe to be true and relevant to your life.

THE VILLAIN DESENSITIZES

There have been some interesting studies done over the years on how the human body can adapt or be "desensitized" to cold weather conditions. For example, in the 1960s, the US Army conducted a study in which they placed soldiers in a 50° F chamber for eight hours a day. The researchers discovered that after about two weeks, the soldiers became accustomed to the cold and (mostly) stopped shivering. A more recent study from army researchers came to the conclusion that all human beings have at least some ability to acclimate to cold temperatures.

How is this possible? Scientists believe a certain type of fatty tissue, called "brown fat," may help the body generate heat in response to continual frosty conditions. Newborns, which lack sufficient muscle to shiver—the body's way of "warming up"—have a lot of stores of this type of fat. As it turns out, people retain some of these stores as they age, particularly around the upper spine and neck. Interestingly, this is why putting on a scarf makes you feel warm. The brain detects cold, in part, according to the temperature of blood flowing through the neck. So the scarf tricks the brain into thinking it is warmer than it actually is.[26]

It is no fluke that it was the US Army that first began conducting this research in the 1960s. Soldiers are often put into life-and-death situations that require them to operate at peak performance if they want to survive. Soldiers who are shivering uncontrollably will have a hard time lining up a target or firing a weapon. This is why the army has a winter training course in Alaska where temperatures routinely drop to -20° F. The soldiers are taught how to operate (and survive) in extreme cold conditions.

Just like those soldiers in the army's research studies or winter training camps, the Enemy is interested in desensitizing you to the climate of the world. Satan wants to make you feel *comfortable* in this world—and with sin. If he can desensitize you so you do not sharply feel the pain of the sin you commit, he can gain a foothold in your life. And, as we've discussed, once he has a foothold, he will try to get you to commit more sins. Such a blatant attack mandates a response. It requires you to put on the helmet of salvation and allow the Holy Spirit to give you a desire for the things of God. It also requires you to pick up the sword of the Spirit and fight back.

1. Think about this tactic of desensitization. How do you know if you have become desensitized to something? As you look back on your life, can you think of anything that once shocked you that you now consider routine or normal?

One of the greatest tactics the Enemy uses against us is the ability to make us numb to the effects and consequences of our sin. When we are submitted to the Spirit of God and we are walking closely with Jesus, fully devoted to Him, and living in obedience to His command, we *should* feel the effects of our sin. We should feel conviction, a desire to repent and turn away from that sin. But the more normalized and habitual the sin is, the less we feel the weight of it. Suddenly, it can become that thing we do or, even worse, who we are. Psychologists have been interested in the concept of desensitization for a while. The premise is quite simple: the more we consume of something, the more used to it our brains (or bodies) become. From a young age, we are formed by what we consume, and this continues on into adulthood.[27]

2. Let's take this idea of desensitization one step further. To what degree do the following vices or negative aspects of your culture make you feel uncomfortable?

Curse words and other forms of bad language:

1	2	3	4	5	6	7	8	9	10

[A bit uncomfortable]   [Very uncomfortable]

Violent scenes in movies or TV shows:

1	2	3	4	5	6	7	8	9	10

[A bit uncomfortable]   [Very uncomfortable]

Nudity or sex scenes in movies or TV shows:

O———O———O———O———O———O———O———O———O———O

| 1 | 2 | 3 | 4 | 5 | 6 | 7 | 8 | 9 | 10 |

[A bit uncomfortable]   [Very uncomfortable]

Seeing other people using drugs or alcohol (in real life or on video):

O———O———O———O———O———O———O———O———O———O

| 1 | 2 | 3 | 4 | 5 | 6 | 7 | 8 | 9 | 10 |

[A bit uncomfortable]   [Very uncomfortable]

3. Read Ephesians 5:3–6. In this passage, Paul reminds us of what it means to put on the helmet of salvation and walk in the light of Christ. In the table below, list each of the things that Paul says you are to reject so that you do not become desensitized to sin.

verse 3	
verse 4	
verse 5	
verse 6	

4. The sword of the Spirit, which is the Word of God, is the weapon you have at your disposal to strike back against the Enemy. Put this sword to use today by looking up the following verses and then writing out what each says about not being conformed to the world.

Romans 12:2	
Ephesians 5:11	
James 4:4	
2 John 1:8–9	

5. Read Philippians 3:17–21. In this passage, Paul reveals both the direction Satan wants to push your life (verses 18–19) and the path God is calling you to walk (verses 20–21). What is one specific step you will take this week to turn away from "earthly things" and instead embrace God's transformation in your life?

CATCH UP AND READ AHEAD

Take time today to connect with a group member and talk about some of the insights from this session. Use any of the prompts below to help guide your discussion.

- What element of this session did you find most important or meaningful? Why that particular element of this session?
- When it comes to the devil gaining footholds, do you feel confident in your ability to evaluate yourself? Are you able to spot those footholds?
- What are some ways that you have experienced a hostility or antagonism toward Christianity or toward your personal faith?
- How would you summarize the process that people go through when they become desensitized to sin, temptation, or rebellion against God?
- What steps are you taking to be mindful of your salvation every day? What steps are you taking so that you can have the Word of God at the ready to counter the Enemy's attacks?

Use this time to go back and complete any of the study and reflection questions from previous days that you weren't able to finish. Make a note below of any revelations you've had and reflect on any growth or personal insights you've gained.

Read chapters 10–13 in *Your Story Has a Villain* before the next group session. Use the space below to note anything that stands out to you or encourages you.

WEEK 5

BEFORE GROUP MEETING	Read chapters 10–13 in *Your Story Has a Villain* Read the Welcome section (page 90)
GROUP MEETING	Discuss the Connect questions Watch the video teaching for session 5 Discuss the questions that follow as a group Do the closing exercise and pray (pages 90–94)
STUDY 1	Complete the personal study (pages 97–100)
STUDY 2	Complete the personal study (pages 101–104)
STUDY 3	Complete the personal study (pages 105–108)
WRAP IT UP	Connect with someone in your group Complete any unfinished personal studies (page 109) Talk with your group about the next study that you want to go through together

ALWAYS BE CONNECTED TO GOD IN PRAYER

And pray in the Spirit on all occasions with all kinds of prayers and requests. With this in mind, be alert and always keep on praying for all the Lord's people. Pray also for me, that whenever I speak, words may be given me so that I will fearlessly make known the mystery of the gospel, for which I am an ambassador in chains. Pray that I may declare it fearlessly, as I should.

EPHESIANS 6:18-20

WELCOME | READ ON YOUR OWN

It's one of the most interesting stories in the Bible when it comes to the spiritual realm and spiritual warfare. Elisha the prophet was being hunted by a squad of soldiers from Aram. The king of that nation had sent the soldiers to kill the prophet because he kept giving Israel's king inside information about Aram's armies and tactics. The soldiers of Aram had hunted Elisha all the way to a city called Dothan, and they were now closing in for the kill.

Elisha's servant, as most of us would be, was nervous about the situation. He cried out to Elisha, "Oh no, my lord! What shall we do?" (2 Kings 6:15). Elisha's response was basically that he didn't need to worry, for the number of troops on their side were far more than on the enemy's side.

Now, keep in mind, the soldiers of Aram had *surrounded* the entire city. Elisha, perhaps sensing his servant's skepticism, then offered a brief prayer: "Open his eyes, LORD, so that he may see" (verse 17). In a flash, the servant was able to see an army of angels surrounding the city. The text says "horses and chariots of fire all around" (verse 17). In other words, the armies of heaven were present and active in that struggle.

The same is true today! We don't have to struggle alone with the villain of our stories. We are backed by heavenly firepower. As we've seen, that starts with the spiritual armor of God. It also includes the sword of the Spirit, which is God's powerful Word. And we also have a weapon called *prayer*. We have the ability to communicate with the God who created the universe—and He has promised to join us in the fight.

CONNECT | 10 MINUTES

Get things started by discussing one of the following questions:

- What is something that resonated with you in last week's personal study that you would like to share with the group?

  — *or* —

- When was the first time you remember praying in a meaningful way? What were the circumstances?

WATCH | 25 MINUTES

Now watch the video for this session. Below is an outline of the key points covered during the teaching. Record any key concepts that stand out to you.

OUTLINE

I. We are called to stand against Satan's attacks by praying on all occasions with all kinds of requests.

   A. "Be alert and always keep on *praying*" (Ephesians 6:18).

   B. "*Pray* that I [Paul] may declare [the gospel] fearlessly" (Ephesians 6:20).

II. It's critical for us to understand there are real dangers in the spiritual world.

   A. Paul has a sense of urgency. He is not admonishing us to be overly frightened, but neither is he advising us to be apathetic. We are to be prepared.

   B. Furthermore, we have to remember that every piece of the armor of God comes from *God*. For this reason, we must stay in communication with God to receive that armor.

   C. We are in a spiritual war—and we receive our spiritual armor and weapons through prayer.

III. Paul advises believers in Christ to "pray in the Spirit" (Ephesians 6:18).

   A. "Praying in the Spirit" means yielding to God's desires for our lives.

   B. It means understanding that the Holy Spirit lives inside us and that He is a part of us.

   C. The powers of darkness hate it when we pray . . . so we must keep praying.

IV. We need to recognize that in spiritual war, we are either advancing or retreating.

   A. Whether we are moving backward or forward in the battle will come down to our prayer life.

   B. Prayer is more than just asking the Lord for things. It is maintaining a *consistent* line of communication with Him—much like a soldier on a radio communicating with his commander.

   C. God is calling us to "be alert"—to be ready for prayer at all times—because we're in a war!

V. Practical thoughts on what it means to pray in this way:

   A. Ask God to fill you with His strength and power.

   B. Ask God to equip you with His spiritual armor.

   C. Ask God to empower you to stand against the villain of your story.

NOTES

DISCUSS | 35 MINUTES

Now discuss what you just watched by answering the following questions.

1. Prayer is one of those elements of the Christian life that we know is important but don't always feel confident in knowing how to make work. How would you describe your experiences with prayer in your journey with Christ?

2. The way we pray is often caught rather than taught. In other words, we learn to pray by watching the examples of others. How has your prayer life been influenced by your parents or your grandparents? How has it been influenced by other examples in your life?

3. Paul challenges us to "pray in the Spirit on all occasions" (Ephesians 6:18). In another letter, he instructs us to "pray continually" and "give thanks in all circumstances" (1 Thessalonians 5:17–18). What does Paul mean when he says we are to pray "on all occasions" and "continually"? What is he saying about the kind of connection we need to have with God?

4. Ask someone to read aloud Matthew 6:31–33. What does Jesus say about prayer in this passage? What reassurance does He give that God will hear us? Why is it important to go to God *first* when there is a need in our life—and not treat prayer like only a last resort?

5. As you come to the conclusion of this study, what are some lingering questions that you still have about spiritual warfare or about prayer that you would like to have answered—or at least addressed? What do you want to discuss before the group wraps things up?

RESPOND | 10 MINUTES

We all experience challenges, and we inevitably figure out ways to deal with them. The problem is that most of the challenges we face are *of* this world: a broken arm, a broken car, a broken bank account, a broken relationship, and so on. However, Paul is calling us to see we have trials of a different kind—those on a spiritual level. Unfortunately, while many of us have become proficient at dealing with earthly trials, we are not as adept at dealing with spiritual trials. We are simply not equipped to engage the Enemy on a spiritual level. This is why we need prayer. We need "spiritual firepower," as Paul explained to the Christians in Corinth and, by extension, to us:

> ³ For though we live in the world, we do not wage war as the world does. ⁴ The weapons we fight with are not the weapons of the world. On the contrary, they have divine power to demolish strongholds. ⁵ We demolish arguments and every pretension that sets itself up against the knowledge of God, and we take captive every thought to make it obedient to Christ. ⁶ And we will be ready to punish every act of disobedience, once your obedience is complete.
>
> **2 CORINTHIANS 10:3–6**

A "stronghold" occurs when Satan gets a foothold that he then uses to entrench himself in our lives. What are some examples of strongholds that are prevalent today?

What promise does Paul provide in this passage for destroying the Enemy's strongholds? How is prayer a key to unlocking this kind of supernatural power in our lives?

PRAY | 10 MINUTES

Conclude by affirming your desire to be in connection with God the Father through the regular, disciplined, and consistent practice of prayer. As mentioned in the teaching, use this time to pray for one another as a group. Specifically ask that God would continue to make known to you the truth about Him and about spiritual warfare as you continue to study His Word.

PERSONAL STUDY

Your story has a villain. As we have seen, he is called by many names, but his goal is always the same: to ruin your life in any way imaginable. He does not work alone but is the leader of a horde of demonic forces that work together across geographies and across generations. This is bad news . . . and frightening news. Yet you need not be afraid. Why? Because you have a Savior. His name is Jesus, and He has promised to be with you and provide everything you need for life and godliness. This includes equipping you to not only resist the villain of your story but also to make him flee. In this final personal study, you will explore one last item that you have in your spiritual arsenal to aid you in the fight: *prayer.* As you work through the exercises, be sure to continue to write down your responses to the questions. If you are reading *Your Story Has a Villain* alongside this study, first review chapters 10–13 in the book.

*Look to the L*ORD *and his strength; seek his face always.*

1 CHRONICLES 16:11

PRAYER ON THE BATTLEFIELD

If you've been in the church for even a little bit of time, you've probably heard some-one say something like this: "God created me the way I am. If He didn't want me to do these behaviors, then He wouldn't have created me with those desires, right? He wouldn't have built me this way if He didn't want me to act this way." Perhaps you have even said something similar when someone questioned you about your lifestyle.

The reality is that we all have innate desires, thoughts, pulls, and instincts that are 100 percent *against* what God wants for our lives. We all have desires to do all kinds of things that are inconsistent with God's values and God's Word. We all have de-sires to say all kinds of things that are inconsistent with God's values and God's Word. We all have desires to avoid all kinds of things that *are* consistent with God's values and God's Word. This is because we were born as a fallen people in a fallen world. We have all been corrupted by sin (see Romans 3:23).

Because of that sin, we experience temptation. Every day. To be a human being is to be tempted to live, speak, and think in ways that are dishonoring to God. This is the bad news. The good news is that we are not hopeless or helpless in the face of that temptation. We have the ability to adjust our desires and change our behavior. In the same way that we can take a stand against Satan and his schemes, we can take a stand against the temptation we experience each day. We do this by staying connected to our heavenly Father through prayer.

The apostle Peter wrote, "[God's] divine power has given us everything we need for a godly life through our knowledge of him who called us by his own glory and goodness" (2 Peter 1:3). We have *everything we need* to lead a God-honoring life. We *can* say no to those moments when we feel pulled toward a particular sin. We *can* reject those larger patterns of sin that have taken root in our lives—those strongholds. We *can* stop making the same mistakes again and again and again. We *can* transform the way we live and the choices we make.

We can do all of these things through the power of Christ who strengthens us!

1. Resisting temptation is difficult for all followers of Jesus, though we don't all struggle with the same types of temptation. To what degree have you been able to resist or maintain victory over the following types of enticements?

How well do you resist the temptation of eating unhealthy foods (gluttony)?

| 1 | 2 | 3 | 4 | 5 | 6 | 7 | 8 | 9 | 10 |

[Not well]   [Very well]

How well do resist sexual temptation (lust)?

| 1 | 2 | 3 | 4 | 5 | 6 | 7 | 8 | 9 | 10 |

[Not well]   [Very well]

How well do you resist the desire to speak harshly or sarcastically (anger)?

| 1 | 2 | 3 | 4 | 5 | 6 | 7 | 8 | 9 | 10 |

[Not well]   [Very well]

How well do you resist the pull of money or possessions (greed)?

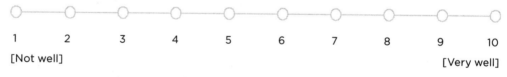

| 1 | 2 | 3 | 4 | 5 | 6 | 7 | 8 | 9 | 10 |

[Not well]   [Very well]

2. In a previous session, we looked at how Jesus resisted Satan's temptation in the wilderness. Read the account of this story as told in Matthew 4:1–11. Notice that it was the Holy Spirit who led Jesus into the wilderness and that Christ spent forty days and forty nights "fasting" in that environment. How do you think this time of preparation (which included prayer) helped Jesus combat

the Enemy's temptations—even though He was weak from hunger? What other spiritual weapon did Jesus employ in this fight against Satan?

On the battlefield, you don't always have time for a strategic communication plan. As bullets are whizzing by, things may not go exactly as you planned. There's no time to huddle up and strategize. You are grabbing your walkie-talkie and giving instructions. You're asking where to go, or telling someone else where you're going, so they know. It's constant and it's practiced often so, in the heat of battle and the fog of war, you are not caught vulnerable and flat-footed by your enemy. Communication on the walkie-talkies is literally a matter of life and death. As the Enemy comes at you with destruction, distraction, deception, disunity, desensitization, and deconstruction to rob you of a life following Jesus, what does your prayer life look like? When one of those six things hits you, how do you respond?[28]

3. Think about this idea that when you are in the midst of the battle—when Satan is throwing temptations at you—you won't have time to huddle up and strategize. All you can do is grab your spiritual "walkie-talkie" and ask your Commander how to overcome. What does this say about the importance of keeping your "lines of communication" open with God? How would you answer this question of what your prayer life today looks like?

4. "Here's a helpful, simple working definition of *temptation*: a proposition to not trust God. . . . It's important to remember that temptation itself is not sinful. The temptation is not what drives a wedge between you and God—sin is."[29] This is an important distinction: *being* tempted is not the problem—*giving in* to temptation is the problem. How do you want to respond whenever you begin to be pulled toward sin (or, as defined here, not trusting God)? What would be your ideal response in moments of temptation?

[12] So, if you think you are standing firm, be careful that you don't fall! [13] No temptation has overtaken you except what is common to mankind. And God is faithful; he will not let you be tempted beyond what you can bear. But when you are tempted, he will also provide a way out so that you can endure it (1 Corinthians 10:12–13).

5. According to this passage, what are some of the ways God has provided for us to resist temptation? What options do you have when you find yourself being pulled away from what is right and toward what you know is wrong?

GUARDING YOUR HEART IN BATTLE

Guard your heart. What do you think of when you hear that phrase? For those of us who grew up in church, these three words might take us back to our high school youth group. We heard those words a lot: "Guard your heart!" Almost always, the words were said in the context of sexual purity. To guard your heart was to refrain from participating in the promiscuity of the culture. It meant reserving your heart for your future spouse rather than giving yourself away sexually (and also emotionally) before committing to a covenant of marriage.

Now, to be absolutely clear, *that is a good thing*. It is certainly true that young people should reject the constant temptation of our hypersexualized society. Yet it's also true that guarding our hearts involves more than resisting sexual sin.

Let's take a step back. Biblically, the command to "guard your heart" is found in the book of Proverbs, which begins with a series of lectures or wisdom statements offered by a father to his son. Specifically, this father was calling out important principles that his son (and, by extension, all who follow God) would need to succeed in life and thrive in God's kingdom.

In the midst of those statements, the father declares, "Above all else, guard your heart, for everything you do flows from it" (Proverbs 4:23). This command is relevant for *all* people of *all* ages and *all* genders and *all* backgrounds. It applies to any person who seeks to follow Jesus in a world that is tainted and corrupted and twisted by sin—especially in a world that is filled with the forces of evil and influenced by a villain who seeks to take us down.

As mentioned in a previous session, protecting the heart is vital because if it is hit by a strike from the Enemy, it could be fatal to us. Perhaps this is why Satan directs so many of his attacks toward our hearts! Most of his strategies, plans, and pitfalls are intended to damage us where we are most vulnerable—at our core. Therefore, we must take every precaution to secure those internal places. We must guard our hearts.

1. How would you define the concept of your heart? (Not the physical organ beating in your chest, of course, but the concept of your heart in the spiritual sense.) When the biblical authors talk about the heart, to what are they referring?

The Enemy loves the unguarded heart because it means you are at your most willing to follow his lead. So, what does it mean to guard your heart? It means that you and I need to be very careful what we allow in. Do we think about this enough? The term Solomon used here when talking about "guarding" is a military term. It's the way that a guard would protect a castle: with violence, hostility, vigilance, alertness, awareness, and a strategy. A guard with that kind of mindset is saying, "No one is going to come into this castle. I must protect it." The instruction here is to *above all else* guard your heart in that same manner. . . . And why do we need to guard our hearts? Because the heart is going to seek what you feed it. It's a very simple idea that you could spend hours and hours meditating and journaling on.[30]

2. Underline this statement in the above quote: "The heart is going to seek what you feed it." What are some of the ways that our culture tries to "feed" the deepest parts of us? In other words, how does our culture try to influence us or develop us at the level of our hearts?

3. Consider for a moment what it means to guard your heart. Use the following prompts to evaluate what you are feeding into your heart on a regular basis.

Ears: "My son, pay attention to what I say; turn your ear to my words. Do not let them out of your sight, keep them within your heart" (Proverbs 4:20–21). Who are you listening to the most right now? Whose words have a big influence on your heart?

Mouth: "Keep your mouth free of perversity; keep corrupt talk far from your lips" (4:24). How do the words you say influence your heart? Do you generally speak in ways that are kind and uplifting or in ways that are harsh or sarcastic?

Eyes: "Let your eyes look straight ahead; fix your gaze directly before you" (4:25). What are the primary sources you look to for guidance, information, and entertainment? How do those sources influence your heart?

Mind: "Give careful thought to the paths for your feet and be steadfast in all your ways" (4:26). What steps have you taken to plan out the path for your life? What are you working to achieve?

Temptation: "Do not turn to the right or the left; keep your foot from evil" (4:27). What are some of the main sources of temptation that cause you to stray away from God's will and God's values?

4. Prayer plays an important role when it comes to guarding our hearts. In the following passage, underline the places where Jesus speaks about *prayer* and *temptation*:

> [39] Jesus went out as usual to the Mount of Olives, and his disciples followed him. [40] On reaching the place, he said to them, "Pray that you will not fall into temptation." [41] He withdrew about a stone's throw beyond them, knelt down and prayed, [42] "Father, if you are willing, take this cup from me; yet not my will, but yours be done." [43] An angel from heaven appeared to him and strengthened him. [44] And being in anguish, he prayed more earnestly, and his sweat was like drops of blood falling to the ground.
>
> [45] When he rose from prayer and went back to the disciples, he found them asleep, exhausted from sorrow. [46] "Why are you sleeping?" he asked them. "Get up and pray so that you will not fall into temptation" (Luke 22:39–46).

Notice that Jesus gave the command to "pray so that you will not fall into temptation" twice to the disciples in the space of just a few verses. What did Jesus understand about prayer that the disciples evidently did not? Given this event occurred right before Jesus was arrested, how was Jesus trying to prepare the disciples for what was to come?

5. How is your heart exposed to the Enemy's attacks? What are some areas that you need to take to Jesus and ask Him to guard? Take a moment to do that right now—believing in your heart that God will answer your prayer (see John 14:14).

STUDY 3

YOU'RE IN THE LORD'S ARMY

If you went to Sunday school for any amount of time during the 1980s or 1990s, or even in more recent decades, it's likely you are familiar with the words of this song:

> *I may never march in the infantry,*
> *ride in the cavalry,*
> *shoot the artillery;*
> *I may never zoom o'er the enemy,*
> *But I'm in the Lord's army! (Yes, sir!)*[31]

There is a lot of truth to that song. When we accept the free gift of salvation through Jesus Christ, we become not just citizens of God's kingdom but also recruits in the battle between good and evil. We become part of the Lord's army. (Yes, sir!)

Unfortunately, many of us believe that wearing the uniform (so to speak) of a soldier in God's army makes us immune from the Enemy's fire. We think that being connected with God through prayer means we are safe from the attacks of the Enemy. So we don't think about defending ourselves from those attacks—and we don't think about fighting back. The truth is that being a Christian means we have a target painted boldly on our backs. Being a member of God's kingdom (or a soldier in His army) means that we are part of a larger battle. We have a responsibility to take action within that fight in ways that resist, deflect, and even engage the Enemy.

In this final personal study, the goal is for you to review everything Paul has said about the spiritual armor of God that you have explored during the past five weeks. As you do this, remember that as a soldier in the Lord's army, you have a mission to "fight the good fight of the faith" (1 Timothy 6:12) and "resist the devil" (James 4:7) so that you can see him "fall like lightning" (Luke 10:18). You are called to stand strong against him, push back his forces, and remove his influence from your life and from the world.

You are called to fight—and you have been given the power from the Lord to win.

1. You have spent the past five weeks in *Your Story Has a Villain* exploring the nature and tactics of your Enemy and discerning how you can resist and fight back against him. What is something new that stands out to you that you didn't know about Satan or the armor of God before you began this study? What questions would you still like to have answered?

[11] Put on the full armor of God, so that you can take your stand against the devil's schemes. [12] For our struggle is not against flesh and blood, but against the rulers, against the authorities, against the powers of this dark world and against the spiritual forces of evil in the heavenly realms. [13] Therefore put on the full armor of God, so that when the day of evil comes, you may be able to stand your ground, and after you have done everything, to stand. [14] Stand firm then, with the belt of truth buckled around your waist, with the breastplate of righteousness in place, [15] and with your feet fitted with the readiness that comes from the gospel of peace. [16] In addition to all this, take up the shield of faith, with which you can extinguish all the flaming arrows of the evil one. [17] Take the helmet of salvation and the sword of the Spirit, which is the word of God. [18] And pray in the Spirit on all occasions with all kinds of prayers and requests. With this in mind, be alert and always keep on praying for all the Lord's people (Ephesians 6:11–18).

2. In the above passage, underline each piece of spiritual armor that Paul says is available to you. Circle every time Paul urges you to stand against Satan and his forces. At a practical level, how do you put on the armor of God so you can stand against the Enemy? What does that look like in your everyday life?

3. Assess your current readiness as a soldier in the Lord's army. To what degree are you covered by God's armor? To what degree are you exposed to the Enemy? Use the graphic below to color in any areas of your spiritual body that you feel are fully protected by God's armor (such as your head covered by the helmet of salvation). Circle any areas that you believe are more unprotected and open to attack.

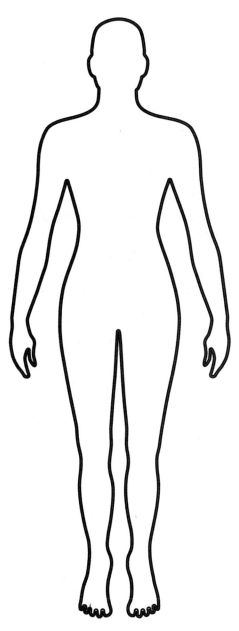

4. Now consider your degree of readiness when it comes to wielding the weapon at your disposal and making sure you are staying connected to your Commander. How confident do you feel in your ability to understand what the Bible says and apply it to your daily life? How would you describe your prayer life? What, if anything, needs to change or improve?

We need to be reminded that our enemy is not the Democrats and it's not the Republicans. The enemy is not your boss, and it is not your angry neighbor. It's not the guy on the road who flipped you off. You only have one Enemy who operates through people to discourage you. If you can just get your head and heart around that idea, you'll fight differently. You'll start to realize, *Oh, this person who just yelled at me and is giving me a piece of their mind with their finger in my chest is not my enemy. There is someone greater than them working through them to discourage me. I have one Enemy, and that is Satan, and the battle is not of flesh and blood.* This is a paradigm-shifting idea for us to understand.[32]

5. Here is a final exercise for you to do as you close out this study. Read Matthew 5:43–48. What does Jesus say in these verses about those who are hostile toward you or even persecute you? How can knowing these people are not your real enemy help you to *do* what Jesus instructs in this passage? What steps will you take in the weeks ahead to not only "love your enemies" but actually "pray for those who persecute you"?

WRAP IT UP

Take time today to connect with a group member and talk about some of the insights from this session. Use any of the prompts below to help guide your discussion.

- What have you found to be the most helpful in this session? What about in this study overall?
- How confident do you feel in your ability to "put on" and use the armor of God each day? Which pieces of that armor are most important in your life right now? Why those pieces?
- Temptation occurs any time you are offered an opportunity not to trust God. How can you identify when those moments are taking place?
- Why is it so critical for you to guard your heart? What role does prayer play in helping you stand against the Enemy and resist the temptations he throws your way?
- How is praying for others (intercession) a part of your normal prayer life? Who are the people in your life right now who most need your prayers?

Use this time to go back and complete any of the study and reflection questions from previous days that you weren't able to finish. Make a note below of any questions you've had and reflect on any growth or personal insights you've gained. Finally, discuss with your group what studies you might want to go through next and when you will plan on meeting together again to study God's Word.

LEADER'S GUIDE

Thank you for your willingness to lead your group through this study! What you have chosen to do is valuable and will make a great difference in the lives of others. The rewards of being a leader are different from those of participating in a group, and we hope that as you lead, you will discover new insights about the nature and tactics that Satan uses against you.

Your Story Has a Villain is a five-session Bible study built around video content and small-group interaction. As the group leader, imagine yourself as the host of a party. Your job is to take care of your guests by managing the details so that when your guests arrive, they can focus on one another and on the interaction around the topic for that session.

Your role as the group leader is not to answer all the questions or reteach the content—the video, book, and study guide will do most of that work. Your job is to guide the experience and cultivate your small group into a connected and engaged community. This will make it a place for members to process, question, and reflect—not necessarily to receive more instruction.

There are several elements in this leader's guide that will help you as you structure your study and reflection time, so be sure to follow along and take advantage of each one.

BEFORE YOU BEGIN

Before your first meeting, make sure the group members have a copy of this study guide. Alternately, you can hand out the study guides at your first meeting and give the members some time to look over the material and ask any preliminary questions. Also, make sure that the group members are aware that they have access to the streaming videos at any time by following the instructions provided with this guide. During your first meeting, ask the members to provide their names, phone numbers, and email addresses so that you can keep in touch with them.

Generally, the ideal size for a group is eight to ten people, which will ensure that everyone has enough time to participate in discussions. If you have more people, you might want to break up the main group into smaller subgroups. Encourage those who show up at the first meeting to commit to attending the duration of the study, as this will help the group members get to know one another, create stability for the group, and help you know how to best prepare to lead them through the material.

Each of the sessions begins with an opening reflection in the Welcome section. The questions that follow in the Connect section serve as an icebreaker to get the group members thinking about the topic. Some people may want to tell a long story in response to one of these questions, but the goal is to keep the answers brief. Ideally, you want everyone in the group to get a chance to answer, so try to keep the responses to a minute or less. If you have talkative group members, say up front that everyone needs to be brief so each person has time to share.

Give the group members a chance to answer, but tell them to feel free to pass if they wish. In the rest of the study, it's generally not best to have everyone answer every question—a free-flowing discussion is more desirable. But with the icebreaker questions, you can go around the circle. Encourage shy people to share, but don't force them.

At your first meeting, let the group members know each session contains a personal study section they can use to continue to engage with the content. While this is optional, it will help them cement the concepts presented during the group study time. Let them know that if they choose to do so, they can watch the video for the next session via streaming. Invite them to bring any questions and insights to your next meeting, especially if they had a breakthrough moment or didn't understand something.

PREPARATION FOR EACH SESSION

As the leader, there are a few things you should do to best prepare for each meeting:

- **Read through the session.** This will help you become more familiar with the content and know how to structure the discussion times.

- **Decide how the videos will be used.** Determine whether you want the members to watch the videos ahead of time (again, via the streaming access code provided with this study guide) or together as a group.

- **Decide which questions you want to discuss.** Based on the length of your group discussions, you may not be able to get through all the questions. So look over the questions and choose which ones you definitely want to cover.

- **Be familiar with the questions you want to discuss.** When the group meets, you'll be watching the clock, so make sure you are familiar with the questions you have selected. In this way you will ensure that you have the material more deeply in your mind than your group members.

- **Pray for your group.** Pray for your group members and ask God to lead them as they study His Word and listen to His Spirit.

Keep in mind as you lead the discussion times that in many cases there will be no one "right" answer to the questions. Answers will vary, especially when the group members are being asked to share their personal experiences.

STRUCTURING THE DISCUSSION TIME

You will need to determine how long you want to meet so you can plan your time accordingly. Suggested times for each section have been provided in this study guide, and if you adhere to these times, your group will meet for ninety minutes. If you want to meet for two hours, follow the times given in the right-hand column.

Section	90 Minutes	120 Minutes
CONNECT (discuss one or more of the opening questions for the session)	15 minutes	20 minutes
WATCH (watch the teaching material together and take notes)	20 minutes	20 minutes
DISCUSS (discuss the study questions you selected ahead of time)	35 minutes	50 minutes
RESPOND (write down key takeaways)	10 minutes	15 minutes
PRAY (pray together and dismiss)	10 minutes	15 minutes

As the group leader, it is up to you to keep track of the time and stay on schedule. You might want to set a timer for each segment so that both you and the group members know when the time is up. (There are some good phone apps for timers that play a gentle chime or other pleasant sound instead of a disruptive noise.)

Don't be concerned if group members are quiet or slow to share. People are often quiet when they are pulling together their ideas, and this might be a new experience for some of them. Just ask a question and let it hang in the air until someone shares. You can then say, "Thank you. What about others? What came to you when you watched that portion of the teaching?"

GROUP DYNAMICS

Leading a group through *Your Story Has a Villain* will be rewarding to you and your group members. But you still may encounter challenges along the way! Discussions can get off track. Group members may not be sensitive to the needs and ideas of others. Some might worry that they will be expected to talk about matters that make them feel awkward. Others may express comments that result in disagreements.

To help ease this strain on you and the group, consider the following ground rules:

- When someone raises a question or comment that is off the main topic, suggest you deal with it another time, or, if you feel led to go in that direction, let the group know that you will be spending some time discussing it.

- If someone asks a question that you don't know how to answer, admit it and move on. At your discretion, feel free to invite group members to comment on questions that call for personal experience.

- If you find that one or two people are dominating the discussion time, direct a few questions to others in the group. Outside the main group time, ask the more dominating members to help you draw out the quieter ones. Work to make them part of the solution instead of part of the problem.

- When a disagreement occurs, encourage the group members to process the matter in love. Encourage those on opposite sides to restate what they heard the other side say about the matter, and then invite each side to evaluate if that perception is accurate. Lead the group in examining other scriptures related to the topic and look for common ground.

When any of these issues arise, encourage your group members to follow these words from Scripture: "Love one another" (John 13:34); "If it is possible, as far as it depends on you, live at peace with everyone" (Romans 12:18); "Whatever is true . . . noble . . . right . . . pure . . . lovely . . . if anything is excellent or praiseworthy—think about such things" (Philippians 4:8); and, "Everyone should be quick to listen, slow to speak and slow to become angry" (James 1:19). This will make your group time more rewarding and beneficial for everyone who attends.

Thank you again for leading your group. You are making a difference in your group members' lives as you help them understand how they can put on the spiritual armor of God each day to stand strong and fight back against the villain in their story.

NOTES

1. Michael Waldron, *Loki*, Marvel Studios and Disney+, 2021.
2. **Satan:** 2 Corinthians 11:14; **the serpent:** Genesis 3:1; **Lucifer** ("the morning star"): Isaiah 14:12; **the devil:** 1 Peter 5:8; **the dragon:** Revelation 12:9.
3. Ligonier Ministries and Lifeway Research, "The State of Theology," https://thestateoftheology.com/data-explorer/2022/20?AGE=30&MF=14&REGION=30&DENSITY=62&EDUCATION=62&INCOME=254&MARITAL=126&ETHNICITY=62&RELTRAD=62&EVB=6&ATTENDANCE=254. *Evangelicals* were defined in the study as having strongly agreed with the following statements: (1) the Bible is the highest authority for what I believe; (2) it is very important for me personally to encourage non-Christians to trust Jesus Christ as their Savior; (3) Jesus Christ's death on the cross is the only sacrifice that could remove the penalty of my sin; and (4) only those who trust in Jesus Christ alone as their Savior receive God's free gift of eternal salvation.
4. Jonathan Pokluda, *Your Story Has a Villain* (Nashville, TN: W Publishing, 2024), 11.
5. Pokluda, *Your Story Has a Villain*, 15.
6. For those not familiar with online shorthand, this means "too long; didn't read."
7. Pokluda, *Your Story Has a Villain*, 28–29.
8. Peter Jackson, *The Lord of the Rings: The Return of the King*, New Line Cinema, 2003.
9. C. S. Lewis, *Christian Reflections* (Grand Rapids, MI: William B. Eerdmans Publishing Company, 1967), 41.
10. Pokluda, *Your Story Has a Villain*, 38–39.
11. "Plate Armor," Wikipedia.com, https://en.wikipedia.org/wiki/Plate_armour#:~:text=Full%20plate%20steel%20armour%20developed,in%20that%20plate%20gradually%20replaced.
12. "The Medieval Suite of Armor," Reliks, https://www.reliks.com/armor/types/medieval-suit-of-armor/.
13. Pokluda, *Your Story Has a Villain*, 50.
14. Pokluda, *Your Story Has a Villain*, 79–80.
15. Pokluda, *Your Story Has a Villain*, 59.
16. "Exoskeletons for the Modern Workforce," The Exoskeleton Store, https://www.theexoskeletonstore.com/pages/exoskeletons-for-modern-workforce?gad_source=1&gclid=Cj0KCQjwmOm3BhC8ARIsAOSbapX4e7hefW4yTSSWYyE-hqdTy36RE2vL_pQzydjL1mGJeKWT18o7pzIaAm93EALw_wcB.
17. Pokluda, *Your Story Has a Villain*, 80–81.
18. Chris Higgins, "Sixty-Five People and Their Famous Last Words," Mental Floss, July 5, 2023, https://www.mentalfloss.com/article/58534/64-people-and-their-famous-last-words.
19. Pokluda, *Your Story Has a Villain,* 66.
20. Pokluda, *Your Story Has a Villain*, 91.
21. "Eleven Fun Facts About Your Brain," Northwestern Medicine, https://www.nm.org/healthbeat/healthy-tips/11-fun-facts-about-your-brain#:~:text=Research%20suggests%20the%20human%20brain,and%20further%20increase%20storage%20capacity
22. Pokluda, *Your Story Has a Villain*, 108.
23. Jeffrey M. Jones, "U.S. Church Membership Falls Below Majority for First Time," Gallup, March 29, 2021, https://news.gallup.com/poll/341963/church-membership-falls-below-majority-first-time.aspx.
24. "Being Christian in Western Europe," Pew Research Center, May 29, 2018, https://www.pewresearch.org/religion/2018/05/29/being-christian-in-western-europe/.
25. Pokluda, *Your Story Has a Villain,* 119.
26. Markham Heid, "How to Help Your Body Adjust to Colder Weather," October 29, 2019, https://time.com/5712904/adjust-to-cold-weather/.
27. Pokluda, *Your Story Has a Villain*, 100–101.
28. Pokluda, *Your Story Has a Villain*, 148.
29. Pokluda, *Your Story Has a Villain*, 161–162.
30. Pokluda, *Your Story Has a Villain*, 174–175.
31. Palmer Wheeler (1905–1983), arranger, "I'm in the Lord's Army."
32. Pokluda, *Your Story Has a Villain*, 134–135.

ABOUT THE AUTHOR

Jonathan "JP" Pokluda is the lead pastor of Harris Creek Baptist Church in Waco, Texas. He was formerly the leader of The Porch in Dallas, which grew to be the largest weekly young adult gathering of its kind in the country. JP didn't come to understand the grace of the gospel until his early twenties after being involved in different denominational churches his entire life. This ignited a desire in him to inspire young adults to radically follow Jesus Christ and unleash them to change the world. JP's wife and partner in ministry is Monica, and together they disciple their children Presley, Finley, and Weston.

JP's bestselling book, *Welcome to Adulting* (2018), offers millennials a road map to navigating faith, finding a spouse, finances, and the future. After that, JP released *Outdated* (2021), which explains God's purpose for singleness, dating, and marriage while covering why, who, and how you should date. His follow-up book, which was written for a broader audience, is *Why Do I Do What I Don't Want to Do?* (2023). His latest release is *Your Story Has a Villain* (2025), on which this study is based.

JP is a popular speaker at many churches and conferences, including THINQ, Passion, and others, and his passion is to share the gospel with anyone who will listen and to equip others to do the same.